T0312050

# Cambridge Elements

Elements in Philosophy and Logic
edited by
Bradley Armour-Garb
*SUNY Albany*
Frederick Kroon
*The University of Auckland*

# PROOFS AND MODELS IN PHILOSOPHICAL LOGIC

Greg Restall
*University of St Andrews*

CAMBRIDGE
UNIVERSITY PRESS

# CAMBRIDGE
## UNIVERSITY PRESS

University Printing House, Cambridge CB2 8BS, United Kingdom

One Liberty Plaza, 20th Floor, New York, NY 10006, USA

477 Williamstown Road, Port Melbourne, VIC 3207, Australia

314–321, 3rd Floor, Plot 3, Splendor Forum, Jasola District Centre, New Delhi – 110025, India

103 Penang Road, #05–06/07, Visioncrest Commercial, Singapore 238467

Cambridge University Press is part of the University of Cambridge.

It furthers the University's mission by disseminating knowledge in the pursuit of education, learning, and research at the highest international levels of excellence.

www.cambridge.org
Information on this title: www.cambridge.org/9781009045384
DOI: 10.1017/9781009040457

First published 2022

A catalogue record for this publication is available from the British Library.

ISBN 978-1-009-04538-4 Paperback
ISSN 2516-418X (online)
ISSN 2516-4171 (print)

# Proofs and Models in Philosophical Logic

Elements in Philosophy and Logic

DOI: 10.1017/9781009040457
First published online: March 2022

Greg Restall
*University of St Andrews*

**Author for correspondence:** Greg Restall, gr69@st-andrews.ac.uk

**Abstract:** This Element is an introduction to recent work on proofs and models in philosophical logic, with a focus on the semantic paradoxes and the sorites paradox. It introduces and motivates different proof systems and different kinds of models for a range of logics, including classical logic, intuitionistic logic, a range of three- and four-valued logics, and substructural logics. It also compares and contrasts the different approaches to substructural treatments of the paradox, showing how the structural rules of contraction, cut and identity feature in paradoxical derivations. It then introduces model theoretic treatments of the paradoxes, including a simple fixed-point model construction that generates three-valued models for theories of truth, which can provide models for a range of different non-classical logics. The Element closes with a discussion of the relationship between proofs and models, arguing that both have their place in philosophers' and logicians' toolkits.

**Keywords:** proofs, models, logic, semantics, paradox

ISBNs: 9781009045384 (PB), 9781009040457 (OC)
ISSNs: 2516-418X (online), 2516-4171 (print)

# Contents

# 1 Context

As far as academic disciplines go, *logic* is strange. In the western academy, its roots go back to Aristotle, to Euclid, to the Stoics, through medievals, the Arabic world, and into a flowering complexity in the nineteenth and twentieth centuries, as philosophers and mathematicians grappled with understanding the power and limits of deductive reasoning. The field we now know as modern logic took root in the project of systematising and securing the foundations of mathematics[1] and in giving an account of the relationship between those mathematical theories and our experience of the world around us. In the twentieth century, new connections emerged with the nascent fields of linguistics, digital systems and computer science. There is no way that an Element on the use of *proofs* and *models* in *philosophical* logic could do justice to anything more than a tiny fragment of this sprawling edifice.[2]

So what small fragment of the discipline of logic will this Element address? As the title states, our focus is *philosophical logic* and the twin roles of *proofs* and *models* in the development of logic. The *philosophical* concern will also be twofold: we will reflect on the application of logic to some questions in philosophy and, at the same time, consider a philosophical reflection on the discipline of logic itself. Philosophical logic provides both a set of sensibilities and processes and tools for application in philosophical discourse (among other kinds of discourse), *and* at same time, it is a site of philosophical reflection. We will maintain these dual perspectives on our topic throughout this Element.

In this first section, I set the scene by way of an introduction to how we can use the different tools of *proofs* and *models* to form judgements about logical validity and invalidity. Then I outline how attention to proofs and models plays a role in some of the current debates in philosophical logic, concerning the *semantic paradoxes* and *vagueness*. I then end the section by looking ahead to the argument of the remainder of the Element.

## 1.1 Proofs and Models

There are many ways to look at *logic* and the constellation of concepts that logicians have attempted to analyse using proofs and models. One way to do

---

[1] J. Alberto Coffa's *The Semantic Tradition from Kant to Carnap* (1993) tells the compelling story of the growth of modern logic beyond its Aristotelian bounds as Bolzano, Weierstrass and others attempted to make sense of the mathematically important notions of convergence and continuity.

[2] So I will not cover the rich tradition of proof complexity, Gentzen's consistency proof for arithmetic, the connections between proof search and decidability and many more interesting topics in proof theory. Neither will I discuss a great deal of model theory, such as significant meta-theoretical results including compactness, cardinality of models or ultrapowers, and other model construction techniques. This Element is only *so* long.

this is to focus on the production and the evaluation of argumentation, reasoning and inference. Let's start with a simple example, involving two mathematicians, who are reasoning about some newfangled binary relation $R$ they are exploring. They have discovered that the relation $R$ is *transitive* (i.e., for any objects $x$, $y$ and $z$ if $R$ relates $x$ to $y$ and $R$ relates $y$ to $z$, then $R$ relates $x$ to $z$ too, so *is older than* is an example of a transitive relation, while *is a parent of* is not) and *symmetric* (if $R$ relates $x$ to $y$, then $R$ relates $y$ back to $x$ too, so neither *is a parent of* nor *is older than* are symmetric relations but *is a sibling of* is), and finally, the relation is *directed* (for each object $x$, there is some object $y$ where $R$ relates $x$ to $y$, so, on the collection of non-negative natural numbers (*natural numbers* for short) $0, 1, 2, \ldots$, the relation *is smaller than* what is directed, since for every number $x$ we can find some whole number $y$ where $x$ is smaller than $y$, but the relation *is larger than* what is not directed if we restrict our attention to the natural numbers. There is no natural number $y$ where 0 is larger than $y$).

So our two mathematicians agree that this newfangled relation $R$ is transitive, symmetric and directed. One of our mathematicians exclaims: 'The relation $R$ is reflexive, too!' (A relation $R$ is *reflexive* if, for every object $x$, $R$ relates that object to *itself*). Our second mathematician asks: why is that? The first responds:

(1)   $R$ is transitive. It's symmetric. It's directed. It must be reflexive, too!

The second mathematician doesn't see why this is the case, so they ask for the reasoning to be spelt out. Can the leap from the premises to the conclusion be broken down into smaller steps? It can. Our quick thinker responds:

(2)   Take an object $a$. Since $R$ is directed, there is some object $b$ where $R$ relates $a$ to $b$. Since $R$ is symmetric, $R$ also relates $b$ to $a$. Now, $R$ relates $a$ to $b$ and $R$ relates $b$ to $a$, so since $R$ is transitive, $R$ relates $a$ to $a$. So we have just shown that for any object $a$ at all, $R$ relates $a$ to itself. That is, $R$ is reflexive.

This elaboration is one way to spell out the jump from the premises to the conclusion. It is what we call a *proof*. It fills out that large jump in thought in terms of smaller steps. In this case, the smaller steps involve the applications of agreed-upon definitions (unpacking the definitions of the terms *reflexivity, transitivity, directedness* and *symmetry*), the operations of individual logical concepts like the universal and existential quantifiers (in the concept of direct-edness, e.g., for *every x, there is some y* where $R$ relates $x$ to $y$), and other logical concepts like conjunction (the *and* in the definition of transitivity) and condi-tionality (the *if* in the definitions of transitivity and symmetry). If you were to question this proof at any of the steps in the explanation, it would seem to be a very different problem than not understanding a large leap in thought. It would be a problem of understanding the concepts in use and not a problem of understanding how those concepts are combined. (That is the idea, anyway. Exactly how proofs work, and what options we have in understanding them is the topic of the next section.)

Proofs are one side of the logical coin. Models are the other. To explain models, we might consider another possible transition in thought: suppose our mathematicians have another newfangled relation $S$, and they have concluded that $S$ is transitive and symmetric, but they do not know whether $S$ is directed or not. They wonder, does it follow from these two properties (transitivity and symmetry) that $S$ is reflexive? We can see that the reasoning supplied previously concerning $R$ does not apply in the case of $S$, since we do not know that $S$ is directed. But having one potential proof that *doesn't* work does not mean that there isn't another proof that *does*. Is it the case that when a relation $S$ is symmetric and transitive, then it must also be reflexive? Our mathematicians think for a while, and sketching some ideas on a blackboard, they draw the following diagram:

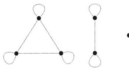

This diagram represents a way a relation $S$ could be. Each dot is a different object in the domain of the relation, and a line connecting dot $x$ with dot $y$ indicates that $S$ relates object $x$ to object $y$. By design, the relation depicted is symmetric, since if there is a line connecting $x$ with $y$ it is line that connects $y$ with $x$. We can see, too, that whenever we can get from $x$ to $y$ and from $y$ to $z$ by lines, there is a direct line from $x$ to $z$. This holds even in the case where we can get from $x$ to $y$ and back – whenever there is a line from $x$ to anywhere at all, there is a line looping around from $x$ to itself. So the relation depicted here is *transitive* too. However, it is not reflexive because we have an isolated dot in our diagram. This lonely object is not a counterexample to the claim of symmetry or of transitivity for $S$, but it shows that if $S$ were like this, it would not be reflexive. We have a *counterexample* to the rule that symmetric and transitive relations must be reflexive.

This counterexample is a *model*. It is not a claim about how the original relation $S$ is. It is a sketch, a representation, showing that if we want an explanation why a relation $S$ *is* reflexive, we cannot appeal merely to its transitivity and its symmetry, since the argument breaks down in circumstances like those depicted in this model. A counterexample is a barrier through which our argument cannot pass.

Here, in a nutshell, we have the distinction between *proofs* and *models*. For the first argument, we have provided a proof, leading from the premises to the conclusion, and for the second, we have provided a *counterexample*, a *model* that renders the premises true and the conclusion false.[3]

The proofs and models we have seen so far are relatively simple, involving reasoning with the quantifiers *all* and *some* and familiar logical connectives like *if* and *and*. There are important questions about the role of these concepts in our argumentation and in our construction of proofs and models. There is broad agreement that these quantifiers and connectives are important. There is less agreement over whether there is anything categorically *distinctive* about those concepts.[4]

➤ ◄

However, there are concepts other than the familiar connectives and quantifiers that have proved important for philosophical logic, and which are amenable to treatment by way of *proofs* and *models*. One example is provided by modal concepts, such as possibility and necessity. However, the proofs and models appropriate for modal operators seem qualitatively different to the models we have seen so far. They do not just represent *a* way things could have been but also represent more than one such way that things could be. To see how they arise, consider the difference between two different arguments:

(3)    It's possible that either $p$ or $q$. So either it's possible that $p$ or it's possible that $q$.

We can fill in this reasoning into a *proof* in the following way:

(4)    Since it's possible that either $p$ or $q$, we grant some possibility where either $p$ or $q$ holds. Suppose it's $p$. In that case, we can conclude that (back where we started) it's possible that $p$, and so it's either possible that $p$ or it's possible that $q$. On the other hand, suppose that the possibility we granted makes $q$ hold. In that case (also, back where we started), it's possible that $q$, and again, either it's possible that $p$ or it's possible that $q$. So, in either case, it's possible that $p$ or it's possible that $q$, and we're done.

---

[3]  Distinguishing validity as defined by way of proofs and validity defined by way of models was a great conceptual advance in the twentieth century. Consult Zach (1999) for a discussion of the early days of that development of the distinction.

[4]  There is extensive literature attempting to characterise the *logical constants* from other concepts. We will not explore it here. Gila Sher's *The Bounds of Logic* is a good place to start (1991).

In this proof, we broke down the leap from premise to conclusion into smaller steps, using more fundamental principles governing possibility and disjunction. This is a good candidate for being a *proof*.

Suppose, on the other hand, we tried a similar argument, with *necessity* in place of possibility.

(5)   It's necessary that either *p* or *q*. So either it's necessary that *p* or it's necessary that *q*.

This argument is less convincing. We can propose a model as a counterexample.

(6)   Suppose we have a range of possibilities, where *some* of them (not all) make *p* true, and the *all the others* (again, not all of possibilities) make *q* true. In that case, in each possibility, we have either *p* or *q* – so from the point of view of any possibility at all, it is *necessary* that either *p* or *q*. Nonetheless, we don't have that it is necessary that *p* (since in some possibilities, *p* fails), and we also do not have that it is necessary that *q* (since in other possiblities, *q* fails). So, in any possibility in our model, we do not have either that it is necessary that *p* or that it is necessary that *q*. So this model, at any possibility, the premise is true, and the conclusion is not.

Modal reasoning works just like the other reasoning we have seen. Valid arguments can be broken down into proofs, while invalid arguments can be given models as counterexamples. The models have a richer structure than the models we saw at first. We used not only a representation of one way that things might be but also a range of such representations, a system of different *possible worlds*.

There are many more concepts that can be rigorously explored with proofs and models, like the identity predicate; definite and indefinite descriptions; quantifiers (over objects) beyond the existential and universal quantifier; quantifiers ranging over other domains, such as *functions*, *propositions* or *properties* and much more. However, this will be more than enough to be going on with for what follows.

## 1.2  Paradoxes

As soon as the field developed accounts of proofs and models – in fact, before these tools took distinct shapes – some natural questions arose. How do we *evaluate* those tools? Do they distinguish good and bad arguments *correctly* (whatever that would mean), or should the main candidates for the correct account of proofs or the correct account of models be revised or rejected? Some of the most active *revisionary* arguments concerning proofs and models have involved different kinds of paradoxes. After all, a paradoxical argument is one where the premises seem true, the argument seems valid and the conclusion seems false. If we want to find a good reason to take some argument that is traditionally thought to be valid to be, in fact, *invalid*, then the paradoxes are where we should look.

### Example 1: The liar paradox

Consider this sentence, which says of itself that it is not true.

(7)   Sentence (7) is not true.

It seems that we can reason like this. Suppose (7) is true. Then, since (7) says that (7) is not true, then it would follow that (7) is not true, which would contradict (7) being true. In other words, if (7) is true, we have a contradiction. This means that (7) is *not* true, since we reduced the supposition that (7) is true to a contradiction. We've refuted it. But this means that we have proved that (7) is not true and that is what (7) itself says. So we've proved (7). It's true. And so, it isn't. We have proved a contradiction.

This is the *liar paradox*, one example of a *semantic paradox*, and a *paradox of self-reference*.[5] As we will see in the next section, we have used very few logical principles in this line of reasoning, and it very much looks like we have made some kind of mistake, though it has proved very difficult to *locate* the mistake to everyone's satisfaction. For some, the semantic paradoxes like the liar have been seen as reasons to curtail our rules of proof for the logical connectives in some way or other, so as to stop the contradictory conclusion or to render the contradictory conclusion palatable. For others, the fact that logical principles like these are involved in the proof means that the problem must lie elsewhere, either in the so-called definition of the liar sentence (say, we attempt to ban self-reference) or to say that despite appearances, the logic of the truth predicate cannot satisfy the rules used here in the derivation of the paradoxes. There are many different kinds of response to the liar paradox, and we will discuss a representative sample of these in the coming sections, since doing so will give us a range of perspectives on what we are *doing* when we use the logical tools of proofs and models.

---

[5]   Another example, which we will also consider, is Curry's paradox, which uses the conditional, where the liar uses negation. Pick some statement $p$. Consider $c$, the class of all classes $x$ where if $x$ is a member of itself, then $p$. Suppose $c$ is a member of itself. Then, it follows that if $c$ is a member of itself, then $p$. So, combining those two facts, we have $p$. In other words, we have just proved that *if* $c$ is a member of itself, then $p$. So, it follows that $c$ is a member of itself. Again, putting these together, we have proved $p$. And we made no assumption about $p$ at all.

## Example 2: The sorites paradox

Consider a colour strip of colour, shading evenly from red on the left to yellow on the right. Let's divide the strip up into 10 000 evenly sized tiny patches, from left to right, labelled 1 to 10 000. For each number *n* from 1 to 10 000, consider the claim that *patch number n looks red* (*to me*). The first such claim, '*patch* 1 *looks red* (*to me*)', is true. The last such claim, *patch* 10 000 *looks red* (*to me*), is false. The claim '*if patch* 1 *looks red to me, so does patch* 2' also seems true, not just because both patches look red but also because they look indistinguishable to me. This generalises: three distinct features conspire to make it that each claim of the form '*if patch n looks red to me, so does patch n* + 1' seems just as true. First, the strip shades evenly from red to yellow, with no sharp changes in observable colour. Second, we chose very many subdivisions, so each patch differs from its neighbours by at most a tiny difference, and third, my powers of visual discrimination have their limits. So the premises of this argument seem true:

(8)   Patch 1 looks red to me.

  If patch 1 looks red to me, so does patch 2.

  If patch 2 looks red to me, so does patch 3.

  $\vdots$

  If patch 9 999 looks red to me, so does patch 10 000.

  Therefore, patch 10 000 looks red to me.

From these premises, we can draw the conclusion that patch 10 000 looks red to me, using one very simple principle of logic, the inference rule of *modus ponens*, which takes us from a conditional claim of the form *if A then B* and its *antecedent A* to its *consequent, B*. Unfortunately, for us, we seem to have a logically valid argument from premises that seem true to a conclusion that seems false.

≻ ≺

If we wish to find a *counterexample* to the validity of the sorites argument, we need to find some model in which the premises hold and in which the conclusion fails. If there is no such counterexample, then either we grant that the argument is valid or we reject the constraint that invalidity must be witnessed by a model as a counterexample. Classical 'two-valued' logical systems have proved difficult to adapt to this task. A two-valued model will assign 'true' or 'false' to each sentence 'patch *n* looks red to me', which will involve assigning either 'true' to each such claim (so this model represents the whole strip as looking red to me) or 'false' to each claim (so the model represents the whole strip as *not* looking red to me), or there are two adjacent patches, and the model represents one as looking red to me and the other as not looking red to me. But, as we said, the set-up is designed to make each patch indistinguishably different from its neighbours. So, if *that* is unpalatable, a natural reaction involves expanding the picture of semantic evaluation to allow for more than the two values of 'true' and 'false': logics with truth-value gaps or a whole panoply of degrees of truth might provide ways to understand the sorites paradoxes. In Section 3, we will examine options for the sorites paradox, as well as other reflections on models that have proved fruitful in philosophical logic in recent decades.

## 1.3 The Plan

The semantic paradoxes and the sorites paradox are two examples of paradoxes over which a great deal of ink has been spilt in recent decades. The philosophical literature concerning the paradoxes provides one entry point – among many – to the different approaches to understanding the foundations of logical consequence, and this is our entryway into the broader landscape of the use of proofs and models in philosophical logic. The paradoxes are sites where what seemed for all the world to be fundamental principles about proofs and about models come into tension and give rise to what seem to be absurd conclusions. Different proposals for revising those fundamental principles or for defusing the tension provide different approaches to understanding these principles of logic, and they will provide a suitable set of lenses through which to view key ideas in logic as they have developed.

≻ ≺

In Section 2, we will discuss logic from the standpoint of *proof*, giving a quick introduction to the kinds of techniques philosophical logicians have adopted in the study of proof and its application to issues in semantics, epistemology and metaphysics. In this section, we will keep an eye on the kinds of responses people have made to the semantic paradoxes, as these paradoxes provide ample motivation for us to inquire into the costs and benefits of different fundamental proof-theoretical principles. Then, in Section 3, we will do the same thing for *models*, introducing not only the debate over the applicability of the standard two-valued 'classical' semantic picture in the light of the paradoxes, but also our sights that will involve discussions of other kinds of models of use in philosophical logic, such as models featuring *possible worlds*, which have proved so useful, and so controversial, in giving an account of the meanings of modal expressions.

After those two sections, we will wrap up with Section 4, in which we explore not only the ways that these tools are used in the discussions of the paradoxes but also some other natural questions, including the relationship between proofs and models themselves. In particular, we will ask which *proofs* and *models* should be taken to be fundamental. But, first, let us turn our attention to proofs.

## 2 Proofs

Let's start with the proof labelled (2) on page 2. That is a *proof* that $R$ is reflexive. It has three premises: $R$ is directed, $R$ is symmetric and $R$ is transitive. It lays out a path from those premises to the conclusion, leaving nothing out. The aim of a proof is not just to convince us *that* some conclusion is true but also, in some sense, to make explicit *how* that conclusion follows from the premises.

Notice that this proof does not just start from the premises and lead to the conclusion, with each intermediate step following from the ones granted before it.[6] There are some other important features of our reasoning that are worth examining. First, our proof includes an *imperative*: 'take an object $a$'. This sentence is not a premise, nor is it a conclusion, and it is not another statement that follows from the premises. It is an invitation. It cannot be true or false. We cannot assert or deny it. Second, the term '$b$' in the proof also has an interesting status. We moved from the claim that $R$ is directed (so, in particular, there must be some object to which $R$ relates $a$) to *calling* one such object $b$. The fact that $R$ relates $a$ to a given object $b$ does not logically follow from the claim that $R$ is directed. $R$ could be directed without $R$ relating $a$ to this particular $b$ (whichever $b$ it happens to be).[7] So much more is going on in this proof than simply working out conclusions from things we have granted. There are different steps where objects are given names, and speech acts, other than asserting, are involved as well. Proofs have complex structure. A crucial constraint, though, is that a proof is not simply a statement of the premises and the conclusion – at least, not in most cases. To *prove* some conclusion $C$ from some premises $P_1$, ..., $P_n$, you must somehow trace the connection *from $P_1, \ldots, P_n$ to $C$*.

---

[6] Proofs with that direct 'linear' structure *Hilbert Proofs*. We will see these in the next section.

[7] If you find this puzzling, think of a concrete case. I have a son. As a matter of fact, Zachary is my son. The fact that *Zachary* is my son does not follow as a logical consequence of the fact that I have a son because there are *other* ways I could have had a son, other than Zac. Similarly, if $R$ relates $a$ to some object, in any particular circumstance in which that is true, we could call that object $b$. Given that choice, it would still not follow that in every circumstance where $R$ relates $a$ to something, that $R$ must relate $a$ to *that* object $b$. It might have related $a$ to some other object instead.

## 2.1 Proof Structures

What kind of structure can a proof have? How can such connections be made, leading from premises to conclusions? In philosophical logic, over recent decades, the focus of research has not been on any general overarching theory of the structure and properties of proofs *as such*.[8] We have seen one example, but in the study of proofs and the formal development of proofs through the years, formal accounts of different kinds of proofs have been represented in many different ways, each with different costs and benefits.

Let's start with the standard logical connectives such as $\wedge$ (conjunction), $\vee$ (disjunction), $\rightarrow$ (the conditional) and $\neg$ (negation) and the quantifiers such as $\forall$ (universal) and $\exists$ (existential) and consider proofs for statements exploiting the concepts in this vocabulary. As mentioned previously, a simple analysis of proofs is given by the structure of *Hilbert Proofs*. A Hilbert Proof from premises $P_1, \ldots, P_n$ to conclusion $C$ is a *list* of formulas, ending in the conclusion $C$, and each of them is (a) one of the premises $P_i$, (b) one of the *axioms* or (c) a formula that follows from earlier formulas in the list by way of the *rules*. Whether something counts as a Hilbert proof depends on the choices of *axioms* and *rules*. If we focus just on the connectives $\rightarrow$ and $\neg$, we can provide a very simple Hilbert proof system for propositional logic. There are three axiom schemes:[9]

WEAKENING: $A \rightarrow (B \rightarrow A)$
DISTRIBUTION: $(A \rightarrow (B \rightarrow C)) \rightarrow ((A \rightarrow B) \rightarrow (A \rightarrow C))$
CONTRAPOSITION: $(\neg B \rightarrow \neg A) \rightarrow (A \rightarrow B)$

These are *schemes* rather than individual formulas because we count *any* formula that fits the shape as an instance of the axiom. So, for example, $p \rightarrow (q \rightarrow p)$ and $p \rightarrow (p \rightarrow p)$, and $\neg(p \rightarrow q) \rightarrow (p \rightarrow \neg(p \rightarrow q))$ are each instance of the WEAKENING axiom scheme. Our Hilbert proof system has just one *rule*:

MODUS PONENS: $A \rightarrow B, A \implies B$

We understand the rule like this: if, in a proof, we have already written down $A \rightarrow B$ and $A$ (in either order), then we can add $B$ to our proof. With this choice of axioms and rules, we can construct proofs in our axiom system

---

[8] See some of Dag Prawitz's papers to see what *could* be done in this direction (1973, 1974, 2019).

[9] Hilbert proofs are named after German mathematician David Hilbert (1862–1943), for whom the *axiomatisation* of mathematics, with a precise formally specified notion of proof, was a central task to the foundation and justification of mathematical methods (see Sieg, 2013; Zach, 2019).

straightforwardly.[10] A proof from a set $X$ of premises to a conclusion $A$ is a list of formulas, where each formula is either an $X$ or an axiom or follows from earlier formulas in the proof by way of the rule and ends in $A$. Here is a proof from $p \to q$ and $q \to r$ to $p \to r$.

| | | |
|---|---|---|
| 1. | $p \to q$ | PREM |
| 2. | $q \to r$ | PREM |
| 3. | $(q \to r) \to (p \to (q \to r))$ | WEAK |
| 4. | $p \to (q \to r)$ | 2, 3, MP |
| 5. | $(p \to (q \to r)) \to ((p \to q) \to (p \to r))$ | DIST |
| 6. | $(p \to q) \to (p \to r)$ | 4, 5, MP |
| 7. | $p \to r$ | 1, 6, MP |

I have numbered every formula in the list and annotated each line with a note indicating the source of the formula. For example, the formula on line 3 is an instance of the WEAKENING axiom, while the formula on line 4 follows from the formulas on lines 2 and 3 using MODUS PONENS.

Recall our motivating conception of a proof as drawing out the connection between the premises and the conclusion, leaving nothing out. Hilbert proofs meet that aim, provided that we are happy to grant that the axioms need no further justification and that the rules of the system are individual steps of deduction, requiring no further analysis. In the case of this Hilbert system, the rule MODUS PONENS seems like a good candidate for meeting that criterion, but the axioms are another question entirely. These axioms look like the kinds of statements that could stand in need of proofs themselves, and this is one reason why, for the purposes of thinking of proofs as laying out justificatory connections as explicitly as possible, attention in philosophical logic has moved away from Hilbert proofs to other proof structures in which there are fewer *axioms* and more *rules*.[11] We will consider *natural deduction* proofs, which correspond more closely to the everyday proof from our example (2).[12]

Here is a short natural deduction proof from the three premises $q \to r, p \to q$ and $p$, using the one rule $\to E$, which licences the inference from a conditional $(A \to B)$ and its antecedent $(A)$ to its consequent $(B)$. Instead of having a linear structure, this natural deduction proof is laid out as a *tree*.

---

[10] The *definition* is straightforward. This does not mean that it is straightforward to find a proof for any given argument.

[11] There are many such proof structures to consider. We will set aside *tableau* (*tree*) proofs (see Smullyan, 1968) and *resolution* proofs (see Genesereth & Kao, 2016) in what follows.

[12] This is a natural deduction in Gentzen–Prawitz format (Prawitz, 1965). There are other ways to format natural deduction proofs, too. See Pelletier's history (1999) for more.

$$\cfrac{q \to r \qquad \cfrac{p \to q \quad p}{q} \; \to E}{r} \; \to E$$

Here, we see that the conclusion $r$ follows from the three premises, which are laid out as leaves of the tree. So far, this is only a presentational difference with Hilbert proofs, but instead of specifying the behaviour of the conditional by adding *axioms*, we add another rule, showing how to *introduce* a conditional statement given a proof. In the previously given proof, we have shown that $r$ holds, given the three assumptions. So, if we grant $q \to r$ and $p \to r$ and withhold commitment to $p$, we can at least conclude that *if* $p$ then $r$. That is, we can conclude $p \to r$. So we have the following two rules for the conditional:

$$\cfrac{\begin{array}{c}[A]^1 \\ \Pi \\ B\end{array}}{A \to B} \; \to I^1 \qquad\qquad \cfrac{A \to B \quad A}{B} \; \to E$$

The $\to E$ rule is straightforward. The $\to I$ rule needs some explaining. It says that if we already have a proof (call it '$\Pi$') with $B$ as a conclusion and with $A$ occurring some number of times among the assumptions,[13] then we can extend the proof by *discharging* those occurrences of $A$ (surrounding them with brackets) and conclude $A \to B$. The active assumptions remaining in the proof are whatever assumptions were active before, except that we *remove* the indicated occurrences of $A$ from that list. So we can extend our previously given proof with one more step:

$$\cfrac{\cfrac{q \to r \qquad \cfrac{p \to q \quad [p]^1}{q} \; \to E,}{r} \; \to E}{p \to r} \; \to I^1$$

to now conclude $p \to r$ from the premises $p \to q$ and $q \to r$. This is a very different proof to the Hilbert proof seen previously, but it, in its own way, shows *how* $p \to r$ follows from $p \to q$ and $q \to r$. One big difference is that our natural deduction proof uses *no* axioms at all (except for the idea that we can assume anything at all – a formula $A$ on its own is a 'proof' with premise $A$ and conclusion $A$), the $\to I$ rule shows how we could *introduce* a conditional $A \to B$ (in terms of its constituents, $A$ and $B$) and the $\to E$ rule shows how we could *eliminate* or *exploit* such a conditional.

---

[13] For reasons, we will discuss in Section 2.3 that number of occurrences can, in fact, be *zero*.

$$\frac{A \quad B}{A \wedge B} \wedge I \qquad \frac{A \wedge B}{A} \wedge E \qquad \frac{A \wedge B}{B} \wedge E \qquad \frac{\begin{array}{c}[A]^i \\ \Pi \\ B\end{array}}{A \rightarrow B} \rightarrow I^i \qquad \frac{A \rightarrow B \quad A}{B} \rightarrow E$$

$$\frac{A}{A \vee B} \vee I \qquad \frac{B}{A \vee B} \vee I \qquad \frac{A \vee B \quad \begin{array}{c}[A]^i \\ \Pi_1 \end{array} \quad \begin{array}{c}[B]^i \\ \Pi_2 \end{array}}{C} \vee E^i$$

$$\frac{\begin{array}{c}[A]^1 \\ \Pi \\ \bot \end{array}}{\neg A} \neg I^1 \qquad \frac{\neg A \quad A}{\bot} \neg E \qquad \frac{\bot}{A} \bot E$$

$$\frac{\begin{array}{c}X \\ \Pi \\ A(n)\end{array}}{\forall x A(x)} \forall I \qquad \frac{\forall x A(x)}{A(t)} \forall E \qquad \frac{A(t)}{\exists x A(x)} \exists I \qquad \frac{\exists x A(x) \quad \begin{array}{c}[A(n)]^i \\ \Pi \\ C\end{array}}{C} \exists E^i$$

$$\frac{}{t = t} =I \qquad \frac{s = t \quad A(s)}{A(t)} =E \qquad \frac{s = t \quad A(t)}{A(s)} =E$$

**Figure 1** Natural deduction rules

In fact, rules of these kinds can be given to the other connectives and quantifiers (they are summarised in Figure 1), and using these rules, we can display the structure of proofs like the everyday reasoning of proof (2).

$$\frac{\dfrac{\forall x \exists y Rxy}{\exists y Ray} \forall E \qquad \dfrac{\dfrac{\dfrac{\forall x \forall y \forall z((Rxy \wedge Ryz) \rightarrow Rxz)}{\forall y \forall z((Ray \wedge Ryz) \rightarrow Raz)} \forall E}{\dfrac{\forall z((Rab \wedge Rbz) \rightarrow Raz)}{(Rab \wedge Rba) \rightarrow Raa} \forall E} \forall E \quad [Rab]^1 \quad \dfrac{\dfrac{\dfrac{\dfrac{\forall x \forall y(Rxy \rightarrow Ryx)}{\forall y(Ray \rightarrow Rya)} \forall E}{Rab \rightarrow Rba} \forall E \quad [Rab]^1}{Rba} \rightarrow E \quad [Rab]^1}{\dfrac{Rab \wedge Rba}{Raa} \rightarrow E}}{Raa} \wedge I}{\dfrac{Raa}{\forall x Rxx} \forall I} \exists E^1$$

Here, the leaves of the proof tree that haven't been discharged are formulas stating that $R$ is directed ($\forall x \exists y Rxy$), transitive ($\forall x \forall y \forall z((Rxy \wedge Ryz) \rightarrow Rxz)$) and symmetric ($\forall x \forall y(Rxy \rightarrow Ryx)$), and the conclusion states that $R$ is reflexive ($\forall x Rxx$). Each step is either an introduction or an elimination rule, operating on a single logical concept, a quantifier or a connective. The rules for the conditional we have seen and the rule introducing a conjunction are straight-forward. The other rules need some comment. The $\forall E$ steps eliminate or *apply* a universally quantified statement by substituting some term (in this case, the terms $a$ and $b$) for the variable *bound* by the quantifier at the head of the expression. In general, $\forall E$ mandates the inference from some statement $\forall x A(x)$ to $A(t)$ for some term $t$.[14] This rule says that from a *universal* claim, we can infer each of its *instances*. The remaining rules in this proof are $\forall I$ and $\exists E$. The last step in our proof is a $\forall I$ step. It echoes the last step in our intuitive proof (2). In the previous step, we concluded that $Raa$, and by this time, the object $a$ in question is *arbitrary*, in the sense that none of the remaining premises in the proof contain the term $a$. We have made no assumptions about what $a$ is, and so the argument applies generally to anything. So we can conclude $\forall x Rxx$. This is the shape of the rule $\forall I$. We can infer $\forall x A(x)$ whenever we have proved $A(n)$ with some name $n$, *provided that n does not occur in the premises X used in that proof*. This move corresponds nicely with the corresponding step in proof (2).

The remaining rule is $\exists E$, and this step also corresponds to a move made in proof (2), though not quite as directly. As we have seen, there is a kind of 'step' that we make from $\exists y Ray$ to $Rab$, but this step should not be thought of as an *inference* in the way that other steps are, since there is no sense in which $Rab$ has to be true if $\exists y Ray$ is true. In our formal proof, the step is conceived of in this way. If we have concluded $\exists y Ray$ (as we have from the premise $\forall x \exists y Rxy$) then to *use* this fact, we can *assume* $Rab$, where $b$ is some fresh name that we have not used before. If we can then conclude some assumption $C$ from that assumption, where $C$ also does not include the name $b$, then we can discharge the assumption $Rab$ and conclude $C$ on the basis of the more general claim $\exists y Ray$. And this is the form of the $\exists E$ rule. So there is a sense in which the statement $Rab$ 'follows from' $\exists y Ray$, not as a valid inference but in the sense that its use as an assumption is discharged on the basis of the weaker formula $\exists y Ray$.

So we have seen that the intuitive *proof* of our mathematicians' everyday reasoning corresponds fairly straightforwardly (after some rearranging) with a formal natural deduction proof in which every step is either an introduction or an elimination.

---

[14] To state this precisely requires an accounting of when a variable in a formula is bound by a quantifier and the substitution of a term for a variable so bound. The details can be found in any good textbook, so we will not pause to give the precise definition here.

## 2.2 Inference Rules as Definitions

Let's return to the idea of *proofs* as making explicit the connections between the premises and the conclusion of an argument. In our original unformalised proof, the basic moves were of two different kinds: they were 'rewriting' definitions of terms of art like 'reflexive', 'transitive' and so on. Disagreeing with any of those steps in our reasoning would have simply been disagreeing about what it is to be transitive or reflexive. Those *definitional* steps are straightforward enough. To accept the definition is to endorse those inferences. What can we say for the other steps in the proof, which, if we are to accept the formalisation in the language of Gentzen/Prawitz natural deduction, are steps like $\forall I$, $\rightarrow E$, and so on. A natural thought is that these steps, too, are in some way distinctive. They certainly look as if they cannot be decomposed into any simpler steps. If we are breaking inferences down into simpler steps, inference rules like these, in which one component of a judgement is operated on at a time, seem like the end point.[15] For proof to not be a thoroughgoingly *relative* or contextually determined notion, or a useless one, there must be some stopping point at which the task of explication ends, and the primitive inference rules of this form is at least suggestive of being the right place.[16] One way that this thought can go further is to take the parallel with definitional steps seriously: to take the connective rules to *define* the concepts they govern. This is a natural thought. After all, we do use rules like $\wedge I$ and $\wedge E$ as one way of specifying what we *mean* when we use the logicians' conjunction (in the same way that we might use the truth conditions of a truth table for $\wedge$). However, this view brings with it some obvious questions. It's one thing to introduce an *abbreviative* definition and to give some account of when it is a legitimate definition. A non-circular definition of a connective may not always be *helpful*, but it will always be a legitimate option. There is no bar to calling a relation $R$ where $\forall x \exists y Rxy$ *directed*. This poses no problems, provided we aren't already using that word for anything else. But our inference rules are not quite like abbreviative definitions, and as Arthur Prior pointed out (1960), not every pair of introduction and elimination rules is legitimate. Prior's argument is simple. If a pair of introduction and elimination rules counts as a *definition*, then what is to rule out defining a concept like *tonk*?

---

[15] For those familiar with model theoretic semantics, inference rules of this form seem to be a natural analogue to truth or satisfaction conditions for each connective, in which the concept being interpreted is dominant and no *other* connective features essentially.

[16] Lewis Carroll's dialogue between Achilles and the Tortoise (1895) is a maddening and delightful example of what can happen if there is *no* such stopping point.

$$\frac{A}{A \ tonk \ B} \ tonkI \qquad \frac{A \ tonk \ B}{B} \ tonkE$$

With the addition of '*tonk*' to our vocabulary, we could reason *from* anywhere (say, from the premise: I exist) to anywhere (to the conclusion: nothing exists) by reasoning through the intermediate step (I exist *tonk* nothing exists) that follows from the premise by a step of *tonk* introduction and from which the conclusion follows by a step of *tonk* elimination. Clearly, this is *too* powerful a tool to use in our reasoning toolkit. Prior took this to be a challenge to the idea that inference rules like the introduction and elimination rules for conjunction count as *definitions*, which may be freely added to our language whenever we please. Rules of this general shape can be powerful – too powerful to be safely added. Some kind of extra criterion must be imposed on our rules if we are to take extending our vocabulary by way of these rules to be the kind of *free* addition typically given by a stipulative definition.

Since it is such a crisply formulated problem, Prior's '*tonk*' has found no small number of responses. One simple and straightforward answer was given by Leslie Stevenson (1961), who argued that connectives like *tonk* are unsuitable because they cannot be made consistent with any truth table. Such an answer takes things out of the orbit of *proofs* and into the domain of *models*, so we will defer its discussion to the next section. Nuel Belnap (1962) formulated a properly proof-theoretic reply when he argued that stipulative definitions – and the traditional inference rules – share properties that rules like those for *tonk* lack. They are *conservatively extending* and *uniquely defining*.

To explain these terms, let's specify the set-up some more. We are considering the addition of some term $T$ to some original language $L$ to form a new language $L + T$. We suppose that our language $L$ comes equipped with a *consequence relation*, formulated in terms of proof. We say that $C$ is a consequence of our premises $P$ iff there is a proof from $P$ to $C$. So, when we move from the original language $L$ to the larger $L + T$, there are not only new sentences that can be formed in our new language but also new *proofs* that can be formulated using our new vocabulary – our new term, $T$. In particular, it may be that we have new proofs from premises in our *old* vocabulary (sentences from $L$) to a conclusion in our old vocabulary (also from $L$), but it makes a detour through our new vocabulary, in $L + T$. The addition of $T$ to our new language is said to be *conservative* if whenever there is an $L + T$-proof from premises in $L$ to a conclusion in $L$, there was originally an $L$-proof from the same premises to the same conclusion.

Stipulative definitions – which add a new vocabulary item to our language by specifying it as a shorthand for some phrase in the old vocabulary – are conservative in just this sense, because if we had some proof in $L + T$, using the new term *T*, we could simply rewrite that proof by replacing all the appeals to the new term by uses of the phrase defining it it in the older vocabulary. The result is a proof in the original language, *L*.

It is plausible that extensions by *definition* (whether by paraphrase, or any other means of defining a term) should be conservative in this sense because a non-conservative extension to our language is more than the addition of new concepts to enable new things. A non-conservative extension is also a *revision* of our view of what holds concerning the *previous* vocabulary. Such an addition to our vocabulary is a revision, since positions that were previously open (granting the premises *P* and rejecting the conclusion *C*) are now deemed to be closed.

Conservative extension in just this sense is one criterion that we could use for distinguishing the behaviour of Prior's '*tonk*' given its rules, and the rules used to define a connective like '∧'. Prior's *tonk* is clearly not conservative over a base language where the argument from some given premise *p* to some given conclusion *q* had no proof, for once *tonk* is added, we have a short, two-step proof from *p* to *q* through *p tonk q*. Can we show that the logical connectives, like ∧, → and ¬, or the quantifiers, like ∀ and ∃, do not fall foul of this criterion? We will see, in the next section, how there is a certain sense in which these logical concepts (in certain contexts) pass Belnap's test, but before we consider that, we should consider the second of Belnap's criteria: *uniqueness*.

Consider a second pair of inference rules, designed to introduce another kind of logical connective, one we can dub '*gonk*'.

$$\frac{A \quad B}{A \; gonk \; B} \; gonkI \quad \frac{A \; gonk \; B}{B} \; gonkE$$

These rules are quite conservative over our usual vocabulary, but they allow for 'wiggle room'. There is nothing in these rules that can distinguish *gonk* from conjunction. If we replace '*gonk*' in our language by '∧' everywhere, these rules would remain valid under this translation, so as far as these rules are concerned, '*gonk*' *could* be just another way to say '∧'. (The fact that *these* rules do not say that we can infer from *A gonk B* to *A* does not mean that this inference *must* be invalid.) Similarly there is nothing in these rules that can distinguish *A gonk B* from *B*. If we replace every sentence in our language of the form of *A gonk B* by alone, *B* and these rules remain valid under *this* translation, too. Our rules for '*gonk*' tell us only that *A* ∧ *B* entails *A gonk B*, and *A gonk B* entails *B*, but exactly *where* between *A*∧*B* and *B* is left unsettled.

It follows that the rules for '*gonk*' are defective in a different way to the defects in the rules for '*tonk*'. The rules for a concept *c* are *uniquely defining* if whenever we define two concepts $c_1$ and $c_2$ using those rules, then $c_1$ and $c_2$ are indistinguishable, using those rules, in the following sense. If $c_1$ is used as a premise, it could be replaced by $c_2$ and vice versa. If $c_1$ is used as a conclusion, it could be replaced by $c_2$ and *vice versa*. Our rules for *gonk* do not satisfy this criterion. Suppose we use the '*gonk*' rules twice to introduce connectives $gonk_1$ and $gonk_2$. If we had a proof from $p\ gonk_1\ q$ to $p\ gonk_2\ q$ using these rules, then we could systematically rewrite that proof using the two translations mentioned in the previous paragraph. Replace $A\ gonk_1\ B$ everywhere by $B$. Replace $A\ gonk_2\ B$ everywhere by $A \wedge B$. The *gonk* rules (in their 1 or 2 guises) are valid under this interpretation, and this means that any proof from $p\ gonk_1\ q$ to $p\ gonk_2\ q$ would become, under this translation, a proof from $q$ to $p \wedge q$. There is no such proof. So, our rules for '*gonk*' do not live up to the conditions of being a *definition*, in Belnap's sense. It fails to be *uniquely defining*.

Concepts introduced by explicit definition are unqiuely defined, provided that there is no equivocation in the definition. So, again, uniqueness seems like a good criterion to look for if we want to characterise *definitions*.

It seems, too, that the usual rules for connectives like $\wedge$, $\rightarrow$, $\neg$ and the quantifiers, fare better than these defective cases. Is there a way to *show* that they do and that the rules are truly well behaved? It is straightforward to show that the rules are uniquely defining. Here is the argument in the case for conjunction.

$$\frac{\dfrac{A \wedge_1 B}{A} {\scriptstyle \wedge_1 E} \quad \dfrac{A \wedge_1 B}{B} {\scriptstyle \wedge_1 E}}{A \wedge_2 B} {\scriptstyle \wedge_2 I} \qquad \frac{\dfrac{A \wedge_2 B}{A} {\scriptstyle \wedge_2 E} \quad \dfrac{A \wedge_2 B}{B} {\scriptstyle \wedge_2 E}}{A \wedge_1 B} {\scriptstyle \wedge_1 I}$$

This shows that concepts introduced by means of the conjunction rules are inter-translatable, at *least* at the level of use as a premise or a conclusion in a proof.[17]

≻ ≺

How could we show that the rules for conjunction, the conditional, negation or the quantifiers are *conservative* additions to any prior language? One way to attempt to show that they are is by way of an interesting property possessed by these rules. They allow for us to eliminate *detours*, in the following sense. Consider a proof where we introduce a conjunction and then eliminate it immediately afterwards. There is clearly a quicker way to get to that conclusion, by

---

[17] Does this mean that they have the same meaning, *tout court*? Possibly *not*. It is plausible that '*but*' satisfies the same inference rules as '*and*' when used as a sentential connective. However, the implicatures involved using a '*but*' instead of an '*and*' are plausibly thought to be a part of the meaning of the word, and not purely determined by the pragmatics, though there is much more to be said there.

refraining to introduce the conjunction in the first place. We get to the same conclusion, and in fact, we need not have used the premises that were featured in the proof of the other, unused conjunct.

$$\cfrac{\cfrac{\overset{\Pi_1}{A} \quad \overset{\Pi_2}{B}}{A \land B}\land I}{A}\land E \qquad \text{simplifies to} \qquad \overset{\Pi_1}{A}$$

The same sort of move can be made if we introduce a conditional and then, immediately thereafter, eliminate it.

$$\cfrac{\cfrac{\overset{[A]}{\overset{\Pi_1}{B}}}{A \to B}\to I \quad \overset{\Pi_2}{A}}{B}\to E \qquad \text{simplifies to} \qquad \overset{\overset{\Pi_2}{A}}{\overset{\Pi_1}{B}}$$

Here, instead of *assuming* the antecedent of the conditional, to prove the consequent, we use the *proof* of the antecedent we used for the elimination step. We insert that proof wherever we formerly assumed the antecedent, and the result is a proof of the conclusion, from the same premises as before. We can do the same sorts of things for other connectives and for the quantifiers.

These are the *normalisation* steps for proofs in natural deduction. Notice that whenever we *normalise* a proof by performing one of these transformations, it gets *simpler* in some sense, by removing formulas that are more complex than those before and after them. These formulas are 'local maxima' in complexity, and they are 'flattened out' in the process of normalisation. The proof does *not* always shrink in this process, since when we normalise some $\to I/E$ pair, the proof $\Pi_2$ of the minor premise $A$ may be large, and it may be substituted into the proof $\Pi_1$ at more than one place. Regardless, it can be shown[18] that for any proof at all using these rules, we can *normalise* it completely so that the result contains no detours.[19]

What does this mean for conservative extension? Each little detour is a place where we made some steps from a premise to a conclusion through a particular concept (some use of a conjunction, conditional, quantifier, etc.) that did not also occur in either the premises or the conclusion. In normalising that step,

---

[18] Prawitz's monograph (1965) contains the proof.

[19] The fact that the process of simplification of detours *terminates* and does not go on forever, might seem obvious, but this requires a detailed argument. The simplification steps – in particular, the steps involving replacement of discharged formulas with entire subproofs, like that for $\to I/\to E$—sometimes simplify a smaller proof involving a detour into a larger proof not involving *that* detour, but perhaps including more detours. To show that the process or reduction terminates, you need to pay attention to the complexity of formulas.

we show that the appeal to that concept in that place is not required. What we can show, in general, is that what happens locally at the site of each individual step of normalisation obtains *globally* in the whole proof, once it has been normalised. We can show that any *normal* proof has the SUBFORMULA PROPERTY in this sense.[20] Every formula in the proof is a subformula of one of the premises or the conclusion of the proof. Normal proofs in this sense are *analytic*, they proceed from the premises to the conclusion by way of the analysis into the formulas' components – no alien material is used.

The consequences for conservative extension can then follow. Suppose we consider the rules for one of our connectives as a proposed definitional extension to our language, containing the other rules. We have seen that the rules for negation are uniquely defining, so one of Belnap's criteria is satisfied. But now we can see that it is conservative, in the following sense: Consider a proof from some premises to a conclusion in our new vocabulary, but where the premises and the conclusion are in the old vocabulary, not using the newly introduced concept. If we normalise the proof, the resulting proof is analytic, and so, since the premises and conclusions do not feature the newly introduced concept, neither does any intermediate step in the proof. So, the proof does not use the newly introduced rules, and so, it is a proof in the old language. Normalisation, in this case, brings with it conservative extension.

So we have some degree of comfort that the logical concepts given by these inference rules share features of concepts introduced by *definition*. They are given an explicit semantics in a sharply defined way, and so, are useful wherever it proves important to have sharply defined and agreed-upon rules. The conservative extension argument shows that introducing such rules does no violence to the pre-existing inferential practice, but adding new concepts can give us new ways to reason with our original vocabulary.

## 2.3 Structural Rules

With this in hand, we can address philosophical issues in and around the theory of proofs, including addressing the *paradoxes* we considered in Section 1. Our argument puts pressure on the idea that the logical concepts are at fault in the paradoxical arguments such as the Liar, since if the logical concepts are given by *definition*, and if they are a free extension of the inferential practice in the pre-logical vocabulary, then there is no point in pinning the blame on the logical vocabulary – the problem must lie elsewhere. So consider these proofs. First,

---

[20]  This is an elegant result due to Dag Prawitz (1965).

a proof that a liar sentence (a sentence $\lambda$ that says of itself that it is not true), is contradictory:

$$\cfrac{\cfrac{\cfrac{\lambda = \ulcorner\neg T\lambda\urcorner \quad [T\lambda]^1}{T^\ulcorner\neg T\lambda\urcorner} {}_{=E}}{\neg T\lambda} {}_{TE} \quad [T\lambda]^1}{\cfrac{\cfrac{\bot}{\neg T\lambda} {}_{\neg I^1}}{} {}_{\neg E}} \qquad \cfrac{\lambda = \ulcorner\neg T\lambda\urcorner \quad \cfrac{\cfrac{\cfrac{\cfrac{\lambda = \ulcorner\neg T\lambda\urcorner \quad [T\lambda]^2}{T^\ulcorner\neg T\lambda\urcorner} {}_{=E}}{\neg T\lambda} {}_{TE} \quad [T\lambda]^2}{\cfrac{\bot}{\neg T\lambda} {}_{\neg I^2}}{} {}_{\neg E}}{T^\ulcorner\neg T\lambda\urcorner} {}_{TI}}{T\lambda} {}_{=E}}{\bot} {}_{\neg E}$$

The new inferences in use are the truth rules *TI/E*, which make use of a *quotation term* $\ulcorner A \urcorner$, for the formula $A$.

$$\frac{A}{T^\ulcorner A\urcorner}\ TI \qquad \frac{T^\ulcorner A\urcorner}{A}\ TE$$

Our second example is the *Curry* paradox, introduced in footnote 5 on page 6. Let '*c*' abbreviate '$\{x : x \in x \to p\}$', a term for the class of all classes such that if they are self-membered, then $p$. We have this proof:

$$\cfrac{\cfrac{\cfrac{[c \in c]^1}{c \in c \to p} {}_{\in E} \quad [c \in c]^1}{p} {}_{\to E}}{c \in c \to p} {}_{\to I^1} \qquad \cfrac{\cfrac{\cfrac{\cfrac{[c \in c]^2}{c \in c \to p} {}_{\in E} \quad [c \in c]^2}{p} {}_{\to E}}{c \in c \to p} {}_{\to I^2}}{c \in c} {}_{\in I}}{p} {}_{\to E}$$

The novel principles here are $\in I/E$, which state that $t$ is in the class of all objects $x$ such that $A(x)$ if and only if $A(t)$.

$$\frac{A(t)}{t \in \{x : A(t)\}}\ {\in}I \qquad \frac{t \in \{x : A(t)\}}{A(t)}\ {\in}E$$

These two paradoxical proofs have *no* rules in common. Regardless, they have shared *features*. One such feature is the circularity or self-reference of the liar sentence $\lambda$ and the Curry class $c$. Perhaps the rules governing truth or class membership should be modified in the presence of such circularity, or maybe such circularity should even be banned. At the very least we should recognise that the $T$ and $\in$ rules are not as *conservative* as rules for the connectives, quantifiers and identity. We can prove $\exists x \exists y (x \neq y)$ using the $T$ or $\in$ rules, even avoiding contraction. The connective, quantifier and identity rules alone do not prove $\exists x\exists y(x \neq y)$, so neither the $T$ nor $\in$ rules are conservative over those rules.

$$
\cfrac{\cfrac{\cfrac{\cfrac{[p]^1}{p \to p}\, {\to}I^1}{[\ulcorner p \to p\urcorner = \ulcorner\bot\urcorner]^2 \;\; \cfrac{}{T\ulcorner p \to p\urcorner}\,TI}\, {=}E}{\cfrac{T\ulcorner\bot\urcorner}{\bot}\,TE}\;\;}{\cfrac{\ulcorner p \to p\urcorner \neq \ulcorner\bot\urcorner}{\cfrac{\exists y(\ulcorner p \to p\urcorner \neq y)}{\exists x\exists y(x \neq y)}\,\exists I}\,\exists I}\,{\neg}I^2}
\qquad
\cfrac{\cfrac{\cfrac{\cfrac{[p]^1}{p \to p}\, {\in}I^1}{[\{x : p \to p\} = \{x : \bot\}]^2 \;\; \cfrac{}{t \in \{x : p \to p\}}\,{\in}I}\, {=}E}{\cfrac{t \in \{x : \bot\}}{\bot}\,{\in}E}}{\cfrac{\{x : p \to p\} \neq \{x : \bot\}}{\cfrac{\exists y(\{x : p \to p\} \neq y)}{\exists x\exists y(x \neq y)}\,\exists I}\,\exists I}\,{\neg}I^2}
$$

Regardless, close analysis of the paradoxical proofs shows that despite the lack of any shared inference rules, there are certain logical principles at work in both proofs, and it is worth examining them more closely.

The most noticeable logical principle in common to both proofs is known as the principle of CONTRACTION. In both proofs, two occurrences of the one assumption are discharged at once. In the liar reasoning, the assumption $T\lambda$ is made twice, to prove the contradiction $\bot$. Both instances are discharged, to conlcude $\neg T\lambda$. For the Curry paradox, the assumption $c \in c$ is made twice, to prove $p$. Both instances are discharged, to prove $c \in c \to p$. If we impose a restriction on discharging assumptions, to the effect that only one assumption may be discharged at any time, then these paradoxical proofs would be ruled out as incorrect. But why would such a restriction be plausible, and what kind of restriction is it?

Contraction is one kind of *structural rule*. It is not a logical inference principle governing this or that connective, but rather, a principle governing proofs *as such*, regardless of the content or structure of any of the statements in the proof. Think of a proof from the premises $A, B, C$ to conclusion $D$ as a proof *for* $A, B, C \succ D$. This structure is called a *sequent*. Contraction is equivalent to the idea that if we have a proof from for $X, A, A \succ B$, then we also have a proof for $X, A \succ B$.[21] Using duplicate discharge, we indeed see that whenever we have a proof $\Pi$ from $X, A, A \succ B$ then we can extend it into a proof for $X, A \succ B$, as shown here:

$$
\cfrac{\cfrac{\begin{array}{c}[A,A]^1 \\ \Pi \\ B\end{array}}{A \to B}\,{\to}I \qquad A}{B}\,{\to}E
$$

---

On the other hand, if whenever we have a proof for $X, A, A \succ B$ we can construct a proof for $X, A \succ B$, then we can get the effect discharging two occurrences of $A$ at once, contracting those two occurrences of $A$ into one by moving from the proof for $X, A, A \succ B$ to that for $X, A \succ B$ and then discharging the single occurrence.

This principle, relating $X, A, A \succ B$ to $X, A \succ B$ involves statements *as such* and has nothing to do with the particular content or structure of any of the statements in question. As such, it is a purely *structural* rule, to do with the structure of proofs as such, and not about the behaviour of this or that connective. It is just the kind of principle that might be lurking in the background, behind paradoxical derivations like those we have seen.

Not only is the structural rule of CONTRACTION present in both of our paradoxical derivations – we can show that if we prohibit it, then adding the $T$ and $\in$ rules to our proof rules for the connectives and quantifiers cannot result in a proof of a contradiction. In fact, a more detailed analysis of proofs can show that in the absence of contraction, there is no *no* proof of contradictions using the logical rules and the $T$ or $\in$ rules. To do this, we can notice that proofs using the $T$ rules and the $\in$ rules may be normalised, too, using these reductions:

$$\cfrac{\cfrac{\cfrac{\Pi}{A}}{T^\ulcorner A \urcorner} \; TI}{A} \; TE \quad \rightsquigarrow \quad \cfrac{\Pi}{A} \qquad\qquad \cfrac{\cfrac{\cfrac{\Pi}{A(t)}}{t \in \{x : A(x)\}} \; \in I}{A(t)} \; \in E \quad \rightsquigarrow \quad \cfrac{\Pi}{A(t)}$$

These reductions differ in one very important respect from the reductions for connectives and quantifiers. The intermediate formulas (here $T^\ulcorner A \urcorner$ or $t \in \{x : A(x)\}$) may be no more complex than the formulas on either side. In the case where $t \in \{x : A(x)\}$ is $c \in c$ (from the Curry paradox) the formula is inferred from $c \in c \to p$, which is *more* complex than the introduced formula. Reducing the proof does not involve cutting out a local maximum in complexity. The reduction simplifies the proof by making the proof strictly smaller but not by eliminating a local maximum in complexity.

The truth and membership rules, then, are well behaved from a proof-theoretic perspective on one measure: normalising these detours shrinks the proof. We've seen that in the presence of contraction, normalisation steps sometimes *enlarge* proofs, but the elegant result we can appeal to here is that if we ban duplicate discharge, simplifying a detour always shrinks a proof, and so, we can totally eliminate detours in proofs, even in the presence of the $T$ and $\in$ rules.[22]

---

[22] In the presence of CONTRACTION, this fails. The paradoxical proofs, given on page 21 are not normal. It is an enjoyable exercise to show that attempting to normalise them results in a cycle.

So, in the absence of contraction, we know that if there is a proof (even using our $T$ or $\in$ rules) for $X \succ A$, then there is a normal proof for $X \succ A$. However, it is straightforward to show that normal proofs satisfy the subformula property (as mentioned on page 20). This has immediate and powerful consequences. There can be no paradoxical derivations of arbitrary conclusions using these rules, since there is no normal proof of an atomic formula $p$ (or $\bot$) from no premises. Since $p$ and $\bot$ have no subformulas at all, no introduction or elimination rules could feature in any such proof satisfying the subformula property. So, the addition of our truth or class rules cannot interact with our logical vocabulary in this devastating way, if we reject CONTRACTION.

$$\succ \quad \prec$$

Once we isolate a structural rule like CONTRACTION, we notice that this discipline of proofs contains other structural rules. Another rule implicit in this system of proofs is called WEAKENING:

$$\frac{X \succ B}{X, A \succ B} \; \textit{Weak}$$

We have passed from the stronger sequent $X \succ B$ to the weaker one. Believe it or not, the rule of weakening is implicit in the conjunction rules $\wedge I/E$. If I have a proof of $B$, this quick detour through $\wedge I/E$

$$\cfrac{\cfrac{A \quad \overset{\Pi}{B}}{A \wedge B} \; {\wedge I}}{B} \; {\wedge E}$$

constructs a proof in which $A$ is now present as an assumption, though it clearly wasn't needed to prove the conclusion $B$. With such a detour, we can construct this proof

$$\cfrac{\cfrac{\cfrac{[A]^1 \quad \overset{\Pi}{B}}{A \wedge B} \; {\wedge I}}{B} \; {\wedge E}}{A \rightarrow B} \; {\rightarrow I^1,}$$

which leads from $B$ to $A \rightarrow B$, where the antecedent $A$ might be totally unconnected to the consequent $B$. The detour through conjunction makes the point completely explicit, but it is not, strictly speaking, necessary. We could get the

---

Either of these proofs simplify to another proof that simplifies back into the original proof. This process can continue indefinitely.

same effect by allowing for rules like $\to I$ discharge *zero* occurrences of an assumption. The proof simplifies to

$$\frac{\displaystyle \begin{array}{c} \Pi \\ B \end{array}}{A \to B} \to I^1$$

Here, the $\to I$ step discharges zero occurrences of the assumption $A$. Such a step is called *vacuous* discharge. So, contraction and weakening correspond to duplicate and vacuous discharge, respectively. If we wish to avoid contraction and weakening, then each discharging step discharges exactly one instance of a formula.

The inference from $B$ to $A \to B$ has been called a 'fallacy of relevance', by those who expect the conditional $A \to B$ to record some kind of connection between antecedent and consequent. Any such connection is lacking here. If we wish the conditional to respect some kind of relevance, it is possible to discard the structural rule of WEAKENING.

It is not hard to see that if we have a system of inference that attempts to keep track of *relevance*, if when the premises in a proof are *used* in the deduction of the conclusion, then we would like to resist WEAKENING. Another reason to resist the rule of weakening is the kind of 'default' inference that allows us to infer from 'this is a bird' to 'this flies', but if we add the premise 'this is a penguin' then the inference is withdrawn. Typically, when considering *deductive* inference, we generalise beyond default inferences to look for inferences that have no counterexamples. The criterion of relevance, though, is less obviously in tension with the canons of deductive validity.

Truly rejecting weakening involves modifying the conjunction rules, since we have seen that they bring weakening in their wake.[23] One simple modification would be to replace the simple $\wedge E$ rules with this:[24]

$$\frac{A \wedge B \qquad \begin{array}{c} [A]^i \; [B]^i \\ \Pi \\ C \end{array}}{C} \wedge E'^i$$

according to which, whenever we arrive at $C$ in a proof in which *both* $A$ and $B$ are assumed, we can instead discharge those assumptions and appeal instead to

---

[23] So, you may notice that Prawitz's result earlier, stating that the traditional rules for conjunction are conservative extensions over the base vocabulary assume WEAKENING over that base vocabulary. If the language did not allow the inference $q$ from $p, q$, then the addition of the standard conjunction rules is no longer conservative, since we can reason from $p, q$ to $p \wedge q$ by one step of $\wedge I$ and then to $q$ by $\wedge E$.

[24] A rule of this form has come to be known as a *general elimination rules*. See von Plato (2001) for a discussion of these rules.

$A \wedge B$. If we allow for vacuous discharge, then we can recover the effect of the original $\wedge E$ rules:

$$\frac{A \wedge B \quad [A]^1}{A} \wedge E'^1 \qquad \frac{A \wedge B \quad [B]^1}{B} \wedge E'^1$$

However, without vacuous dischgarge, the new $\wedge E'$ rule differs from its alternative, and it is a genuinely different treatment of conjunction that respects relevance constraints.

There are two more structural rules that will be important in our discussions of the paradoxes, proofs and models. WEAKENING and CONTRACTION concern the behaviour of premise combination. The rules of IDENTITY and CUT focus on the relationships between premises and conclusions:

$$A \succ A \quad Id \qquad \frac{X \succ A \quad Y, A \succ B}{X, Y \succ B} \quad Cut$$

Restricting the paradoxical arguments at the point of CONTRACTION is elegant and uniform, but it comes with its own costs. For one, we appeal to duplicate discharge *everywhere* in our reasoning, not only in paradoxical settings Ripley (2015b). So, friends of contraction-free approaches to the paradoxes have attempted to show how one might reincorporate contraction in safe non-paradoxical settings, with limited success (Petersen, 2000, 2003). Another, perhaps more fundamental concern, is philosophical. What does the single discharge restriction *mean*? We are not used to accounting for our premises down to the *use*, and it is not clear that such an accounting coheres with what we are doing when we assert and deny. After all when we assert, one license we grant is for others to *re*-assert that claim on the basis of *our* assertion (Brandom, 1983; Lackey, 2007). It would be strange if that right was not even extended to ourselves, and the assumptions we make.

We can make one preliminary conclusion. When we look at paradoxical proofs, we can see that CONTRACTION playing some kind of role. Exploring proof systems that limit the use of contraction looks like one natural way to respond to the paradoxes. However, incorporating this approach into a wider account of what it is to assert, infer and reason – and giving some account of when contraction fails – requires more work (Zardini, 2011).

We will turn our attention to other ways to respond to the paradoxes, inspired by attention to the structure of the paradoxical proofs. Before we can dive into those details, we need to address one further question about our inference rules, and our assumptions about the structure of proofs in which those inference rules are framed. And one way that this question could be asked starts with the rules for *negation*.

➤ ➤

Consider our rules for negation. We have a simple proof from $p$ to its double negation, $\neg\neg p$:

$$\frac{\dfrac{[\neg p]^1 \quad p}{\bot} \, \neg E}{\neg\neg p} \, \neg I$$

Could we reverse the inference to find a proof from $\neg\neg p$ to $p$? It turns out that the answer is: *no, so far*. There is no proof, using our natural deduction rules, that will lead us from the premise $\neg\neg p$ to conclude $p$.

What does this say about the argument from $\neg\neg p$ to $p$? Is it valid? (We can defer discussion of the question of whether it has a *counterexample* to the next section.) If it is valid, what kind of *proof* could lead us from $\neg\neg p$ to $p$? Certainly the kind of truth tables familiar from elementary logic classes would tell us that the argument *is* valid, so finding a proof would seem like a pressing task. What are the fundamental features concerning negation that lead us from $\neg\neg p$ to $p$?

There are at least three different responses to this challenge. The first is to refuse it. To agree with the verdict of our proof system and to say that the argument is, in fact, invalid. This is the response of the *intuitionist* (Brouwer, 1913; Dummett, 1977; van Dalen, 1986). The inference rules defining negation are strong enough to sustain the principles of intuitionistic logic and no more.

The second approach is to add some principle to bridge the gap. For example, adding the inference of double negation elimination by itself:

$$\frac{\neg\neg A}{A} \, DNE$$

or something like this 'reductio' principle:

$$\begin{array}{c} [\neg A]^i \\ \Pi \\ \dfrac{\bot}{A} \, Reductio^i \end{array}$$

would suffice. Adding an *extra* rule like this comes at some cost to the idea that the inference rules are definitions. For example, using any of these principles we can prove Peirce's Law:

$$\frac{\dfrac{\dfrac{\dfrac{[\neg p]^2 \quad [p]^1}{\dfrac{\bot}{q} \, \bot E}}{p \to q} \to I^1}{p} \neg E}{\dfrac{\bot}{\neg\neg p} \neg I^i}$$

$$\frac{(p \to q) \to p \qquad p \to q}{\dfrac{p}{\dfrac{\bot}{\neg\neg p} \neg I^i}} \neg E$$

$$\frac{[\neg p]^2}{\dfrac{\dfrac{p}{\dfrac{\bot}{\neg\neg p} \neg I^i}}{\dfrac{p}{((p \to q) \to p) \to p} \to I^2} DNE}$$

However, there is no proof of $((p \to q) \to p) \to p$ in our original system. So, if our aim is to have an account of the logical principles that count as *definitions*, then it seems that either the definition for '$\to$' is incomplete without supplementation or the addition of extra rules for negation is an overreach.

Nonetheless, all is not lost. An insight from Gerhard Gentzen can give us an alternative way to understand the underlying framework of inference, so that the *existing* inference rules suffice to define the logical concepts. Gentzen's insight is that when we put the rules in an appropriately wider context, there will be new ways to combine those rules, resulting in proofs from $\neg\neg p$ to $p$, to prove $((p \to q) \to p) \to p$ and more.

To understand that insight of Gentzen's, we must take a step back from natural deduction proofs to keep track of the *score* at each step of a proof. A proof (so far, at least) always leads from some collection $X$ (possibly empty) of premises to some conclusion $A$. We can represent the 'score' in what we call a *sequent*, a structure the form $X \succ A$. As a proof is developed, the score changes. The short proof that consists of the assumption $p$ corresponds to the sequent

$$p \succ p$$

in which the $p$ is both an assumption and the conclusion. As you read the proof from $p$ to $\neg\neg p$ from top to bottom, you can see the *score* develop in parallel:

$$\frac{[\neg p]^1 \quad p}{\dfrac{\bot}{\neg\neg p} \neg I} \neg E \qquad\qquad \frac{\dfrac{p \succ p}{p, \neg p \succ} \neg L}{p \succ \neg\neg p} \neg R$$

In this 'sequent derivation' you can see two principles at work:

$$\frac{X \succ A}{X, \neg A \succ \bot} \neg L \qquad\qquad \frac{X, A \succ \bot}{X \succ \neg A} \neg R$$

If you can prove a contradiction from $X$ and $A$, then we can prove $\neg A$ from $X$ ('blaming' the contradiction on $A$). On the other hand, if we can prove $A$ from $X$, then $X$ together with $\neg A$ would be contradictory. For Gentzen, we can represent contradictoriness in a *sequent* by leaving out the $\perp$ formula. The rules have this shape:

$$\frac{X \succ A}{X, \neg A \succ} \neg L \qquad \frac{X, A \succ}{X \succ \neg A} \neg R$$

where a sequent of the form $X \succ$ indicates the fact that the assumptions $X$ are contradictory. The negation rules swap the formula from one side of the sequent to the other. Gentzen's insight was that one could make a very simple modification to these sequents to allow properly classical proofs without adding ad hoc extra principles. All we need to do is to liberate sequents from the shape $X \succ A$ (or $X \succ$), to include more than one formula on the right hand side, too. Then, the negation rules would take the shape as follows:

$$\frac{X \succ A, Y}{X, \neg A \succ Y} \neg L \qquad \frac{X, A \succ Y}{X \succ \neg A, Y} \neg R$$

and our derivation of $p \succ \neg\neg p$ has a natural mirror image, a derivation of $\neg\neg p \succ p$.

$$\frac{\dfrac{p \succ p}{p, \neg p \succ} \neg L}{p \succ \neg\neg p} \neg R \qquad \frac{\dfrac{p \succ p}{\succ p, \neg p} \neg R}{\neg\neg p \succ p} \neg L$$

The rules for the conditional generalise in the following way, where the only change from the original setting is that we allow for more than one formula on the right hand side.

$$\frac{X \succ A, Y \qquad X', B \succ Y'}{X, A \to B, X' \succ Y, Y'} \to L \qquad \frac{X, A \succ B, Y}{X \succ A \to B, Y} \to R$$

The extra 'room to move' allowed in a derivation with more than one formula in the right hand side provides a derivation of Peirce's Law, without any detour through negation:[25]

$$\frac{\dfrac{\dfrac{\dfrac{\dfrac{p \succ p}{p \succ p, q} \text{ Weakening}}{\succ p, p \to q} \to R \qquad p \succ p}{\dfrac{(p \to q) \to p \succ p, p}{(p \to q) \to p \succ p} \text{ Contraction}}}{\succ ((p \to q) \to p) \to p} \to R}{}$$

There is no doubt that sequent derivations of this form are an elegant and powerful representation of some kind of 'provability' in classical logic. However,

---

[25] Notice that there are two explicit appeals to structural rules in this derivation. One step of *weakening* adds a $q$ in conclusion position, and another *contraction* in conclusion position transforms two instances of $p$ into one. These are naturally 'dual' to the structural rules on the left hand side of the sequent.

the question must be asked: is this just a *trick*, with no real interpretation (Milne, 2002)? After all, sequents of the form $X \succ A$ have a real *meaning* given in terms of proof. The derivation of a sequent of the form $X \succ A$ indicates that there is a proof from $X$ to $A$. What does the sequent $\succ p, \neg p$ represent? It cannot mean that there is a proof of either $p$ or of $\neg p$, since there is no such proof (Steinberger, 2011).

One possible response is to say that a derivation of $X \succ Y$ indicates that it is *out of bounds* to assert each member of $X$ and to deny each member of $Y$ (Restall, 2005). This makes sense of the derivation of $\succ p, \neg p$, since indeed, there seems to be a mistake involved in denying both $p$ and $\neg p$—after all, our grounds for *denying p* in the relevant sense, seem to be grounds for asserting $\neg p$. This matches the interpretation of $p, \neg p \succ$, which tells us that it is out of bounds to assert $p$ and to assert $\neg p$—after all, our grounds for *asserting* $\neg p$, in the relevant sense, seem to be grounds for denying $p$.

More could be said about the assertion/denial interpretation of '$X \succ Y$' sequents, but we should be aware of one important criticism that has been repeatedly made: this interpretation must be supplemented with at least *some* account of *inference*, if it is to have any connection with the original interpretation of sequents, for which a sequent represents a proof *from* premises *to* a conclusion. After all, we don't want the merely negative result that a derivation of $X \succ A$ tells us that it would be a mistake to assert each member of $X$ and to deny $A$, without also saying at least something concerning what we could *do*, were we to grant each member of $X$. One thing that the *proof* interpretation tells us is that we could *conclude A*. The assertion/denial interpretation does not make this connection, at least, not without further interpretive work.

Whatever we may say about that criticism, the point remains that the interpretation of sequents in terms of constraints on assertion and denial are independently compelling, and they may be explored independently of any *immediate* connection to natural deduction proof. With that connection in mind, let's reconstruct our paradoxical derivations in a sequent setting. To do this, we need to use not only sequent rules for our connectives, but also consider the rules for $\in$ and $T$. These have natural left/right forms in sequents, corresponding to the elimination and introduction natural deduction rules:

$$\frac{X, A \succ Y}{X, T^\ulcorner A^\urcorner \succ Y}\ TL \qquad \frac{X \succ A, Y}{X \succ T^\ulcorner A^\urcorner, Y}\ TR$$

$$\frac{X, A(t) \succ Y}{X, t \in \{x : A(t)\} \succ Y}\ \in L \qquad \frac{X \succ A(t), Y}{X \succ t \in \{x : A(t)\}, Y}\ \in R$$

For Curry's paradox, we start with this derivation of $c \in c \succ p$.

$$\cfrac{\cfrac{c \in c \to p \succ c \in c \to p}{c \in c \succ c \in c \to p}\ {\in}L \qquad \cfrac{c \in c \succ c \in c \qquad p \succ p}{c \in c, c \in c \to p \succ p}\ {\to}L}{\cfrac{\cfrac{c \in c, c \in c \succ p}{c \in c \succ p}\ \text{Contraction}}{}}\ \text{Cut}$$

(Notice that it uses a *Cut*.) If we call that derivation $\Delta$, we can extend it as follows:

$$\cfrac{\cfrac{\cfrac{\Delta}{c \in c \succ p}}{\cfrac{\succ c \in c \to p}{\succ c \in c}\ {\in}R}\ {\to}R \qquad \cfrac{\Delta}{c \in c \succ p}}{\succ p}\ \text{Cut}$$

For the liar paradox, the derivation has a similar structure. Start with this derivation of $\lambda = \ulcorner \neg T\lambda \urcorner \succ \neg T\lambda$.

$$\cfrac{\cfrac{\cfrac{T\lambda \succ T\lambda}{\lambda = \ulcorner \neg T\lambda \urcorner, T\lambda \succ T \ulcorner \neg T\lambda \urcorner}\ {=}L \qquad \cfrac{\neg T\lambda \succ \neg T\lambda}{T\ulcorner \neg T\lambda \urcorner \succ \neg T\lambda}\ TL}{\cfrac{\cfrac{\lambda = \ulcorner \neg T\lambda \urcorner, T\lambda \succ \neg T\lambda}{\lambda = \ulcorner \neg T\lambda \urcorner \succ \neg T\lambda, \neg T\lambda}\ {\neg}R}{\lambda = \ulcorner \neg T\lambda \urcorner \succ \neg T\lambda}\ \text{Contraction}}}{}}{}\ \text{Cut}$$

and we'll call this $\Delta'$. (Notice that this derivation uses a contraction on the *right* of the sequent, in addition to a *Cut*.) We can extend the derivation as follows:

$$\cfrac{\cfrac{\Delta'}{\lambda = \ulcorner \neg T\lambda \urcorner \succ \neg T\lambda} \qquad \cfrac{\cfrac{\cfrac{\cfrac{\cfrac{\Delta'}{\lambda = \ulcorner \neg T\lambda \urcorner \succ \neg T\lambda}}{\lambda = \ulcorner \neg T\lambda \urcorner \succ T \ulcorner \neg T\lambda \urcorner}\ TR}{\cfrac{\lambda = \ulcorner \neg T\lambda \urcorner, \lambda = \ulcorner \neg T\lambda \urcorner \succ T\lambda}{\lambda = \ulcorner \neg T\lambda \urcorner \succ T\lambda}\ \text{Contraction}}\ {=}L}{\lambda = \ulcorner \neg T\lambda \urcorner, \neg T\lambda \succ}\ {\neg}L}{}}{\cfrac{\cfrac{\lambda = \ulcorner \neg T\lambda \urcorner, \lambda = \ulcorner \neg T\lambda \urcorner \succ}{\lambda = \ulcorner \neg T\lambda \urcorner \succ}\ \text{Contraction}}{}}\ \text{Cut}}{}$$

Here, truth, membership, identity and the connectives are governed by left and right rules instead of introduction and elimination rules. As before, we can see the role of contraction, though here it is a separate inference rule. Two other structural rules loom into focus. The more obvious is the CUT rule, and the second is the IDENTITY axiom $A \succ A$, appealed to at each leaf of the tree.

We have already seen that IDENTITY and CUT are structural rules, since they act on any formula whatsoever, and make no appeal to the content of a formula. In terms of the bounds, the IDENTITY rule states that it is out of bounds to assert

*A* and deny *A*. The CUT rule is a little more complex: read from top to bottom, it tells us that if it is out of bounds to assert each member of *X* and *deny A* and deny each member of *Y*, and it is also out of bounds to assert each member of *X* and *assert A* and deny each member of *Y*, then the problem, as it were, lies with asserting each member of *X* and denying each member of *Y*, rather than with *A*. To read this contrapositively, it tells us that if it is *in* bounds to assert each member of *X* and deny each member of *Y*, then either adding *A* as an assertion is in bounds, or adding *A* as a denial is in bounds.

The two rules of CUT and IDENTITY have themselves faced the harsh glare of judgement, since they – like contraction – are *also* exposed as common factors in paradoxical proofs. Consider *Cut*: Why is this a suspect? If the *Cut* formula is paradoxical, then we may well think that a position may be in bounds, but adding that paradoxical statement an assertion may be out of bounds (after all, if I assert $T\lambda$ then I should deny it as well) and adding it as a denial is also out of bounds (after all, if I deny $T\lambda$ then this is grounds for asserting it). This seems like a good reason to explore going without the *Cut* rule, at least in its full generality.

Doing without *Cut* may be more straightforward than it might appear, because it has been shown that as far as *logic* is concerned, there is no requirement to appeal to *Cut* in the derivation of a sequent (Gentzen, 1935a,b, 1969), since any sequent $X \succ Y$ that be derived using *Cut* can be derived without it. (*Cut* elimination, in the sequent calculus, corresponds closely to normalisation in natural deduction.) So far, so good. However, *Cut* is everywhere as far as logic is *applied*. We may have derivations of $T \succ A$ and of $T \succ A \rightarrow B$, where *T* is some given background theory, and *A* and $A \rightarrow B$ are consequences of that theory. In the absence of *Cut*, we cannot conclude that *B* also folows from *T*. We cannot, in general, chain statements about the bounds together in this way.

In the absence of *Cut*, paradoxical concepts like naïve truth and class membership are *safe*, in the sense that they do not allow for the derivation of paradoxical consequences, but there is an important sense in which they are *inert*. We cannot get far, using them, in the absence of *Cut*. And not only the paradoxical concepts themselves, but also the whole vocabulary, unless we impose *Cut* for other vocabulary items that are taken to be 'safe'.

This problem becomes more acute when we raise the issue, stated previously, concerning the connection between this approach to the bounds on assertion and denial and our initial concern for *proof*. If we think of a proof as licensing an *inference*, in the sense of meeting a justification request for an assertion, against the context of other assertions taken for granted (so, a proof from *X* to *A* shows you how to meet the justification request for an assertion of *A*, appealing only to the premises *X*), then the issue of the validity or the invalidity of *Cut* becomes the issue of the composition of proofs, or the chaining together of inferences. To put the question more starkly: if we are to resist the paradoxical inferences by objecting to the *Cut* steps in our previously mentioned derivations, then the corresponding move when it comes to the natural deduction *proofs* seems downright weird. We grant the proof from *A* to *B* and we grant the proof from *B* to *C* but we resist chaining them together. This puts severe pressure on the usual interpretation of natural deduction proofs, especially when we conceive of them as the meeting of justification requests. If a proof from *A* to *B* shows how I can justify the claim *B* by appeal to *A*, and a proof from *B* to *C* shows how I can justify the claim *C* by appeal to *B*, then where has the obvious justification of *C* on the basis of *A* – by first justifying *B*, and then on the basis of that, justifying *C* – broken down? Breaking the proof at the *Cut* step means that either we reject the sense in which we can use proofs to accumulate commitments, making explicit what was implicit in what we have initially granted, or we must find some *other* way to make sense of this form of accumulation and composition of proofs.

> ≻ ≺

I indicated that the sequent derivation perspective on our paradoxical proofs provides one other culprit. That culprit is not found at any step in the middle of the derivation, but at the *leaves*. The *Id* steps in our proofs are the simplest starting points: the atomic sequents from which all others follow. If we reject the *Cut* steps because we took paradoxical claims like the liar to be both unassertible and undeniable (a kind of *gap*), then the dual perspective, taking the paradoxical sentences to be both assertible and deniable (a kind of *glut*) would direct us to have never started the derivation in the first place, for a sequent like $A \succ A$ fails to hold in the case where *A* is paradoxical: it need not be out of bounds to both assert the liar sentence and deny it. In that case, the paradoxical derivation does not get off the ground, because the identity sequent is not, in general, valid. On this interpretation of the state of affairs, the *Cut* rule need not raise any problems, since the issue is not that the liar sentence is too problematic to assert or deny. It is rather that it is too accommodating to be ruled out. There is no doubt that this interpretation of sequents allows for a distinctive way to block the derivation. If we are not allowed to *start*, there is no way to derive our problematic conclusion. Of course, in our sequent system, the identity axiom is the *only* axiom, so we cannot prove *anything*, other than *doubly conditional* conclusions. Our sequents are already, in some sense, conditional claims, and now we cannot prove any sequent in a categorical sense, but we can prove them conditionally, in the sense that (for example) *if* $X, A \succ B, Y$ *were out of bounds*, so would $X, \neg B \succ \neg A, Y$. (Of course, we could posit *particular* axioms governing particular vocabulary, taken to be safe, in the same way that the opponent of *Cut* might impose particular instances of the *Cut* rule in just this sense.)[26]

If the issue of the interpretation of *proofs* was sharp in the case of rejecting *Cut*, it is equally sharp, if not more so, in the case of rejecting *Identity*. To what does the rejection of *Id* correspond in natural deduction proofs? It corresponds to refusing to start in the first place. In the natural deduction setting, rejecting the axiom of identity corresponds to rejecting the making of assumptions, for the identity sequent $A \succ A$ corresponds to the natural deduction proof consisting of the assumption of $A$, which is at the very same time the premise and the conclusion of the proof.

What reason might we have for rejecting this principle? In the sequent setting, we reject $A \succ A$ in the case where it might be in bounds to both accept and to reject $A$, to assert it and to deny it at the very same time. In this case, we may understand an atomic proof involving the single formula $A$ as defective because it does not *constrain* assertion and denial in the right way. If a proof from $P$ to $C$ is to show that it is out of bounds to assert the premises and deny the conclusion, then the so-called proof with premise $A$ and conclusion $A$ fails. Since, on this view, it is in bounds to both assert $A$ and to deny it, $A$ should not occur on its own as an atomic proof.

## 2.4 Other Proof Structures

There is much more that could be said about the application of proof-theoretical techniques to the paradoxes, but before we finish this section, we will turn aside to *briefly* consider proof-theoretical treatments of concepts beyond the familiar logical connectives of conjunction, negation, the conditional and the like. We have already seen the quantifiers, when we briefly discussed the role of the universal quantifier introduction rule on page 14. You can see, when comparing this inference rule to the connective rules, that quantifier rules involve an analysis of sentences in our language in terms of predicates and singular terms, and some notion of substitution of one term for another. The rules only make sense relative to such an analysis. Proofs involving quantifiers involve a new kind of structure, at the level of the formulas inside the proofs, when compared to proofs involving the usual propositional connectives.[27]

---

[26] See French (2016) for a further discussion of the issues surrounding the rejection of *Identity* in sequent systems and the interpretation of the semantic paradoxes.

[27] There are options to consider when it comes to quantifier rules like $\forall I/E$ and $\exists I/E$. One choice worth considering is whether our language allows for so-called *undefined* terms, and if so, whether they can feature in inferences such as $\forall E$ and $\exists I$. In a mathematical language in which it is appropriate to make claims such as $\frac{1}{0}$ is not defined, would it be appropriate to conclude:

Let's briefly consider other concepts that are amenable to a logical analysis: modal operators. The concepts of possibility and necessity have been subjected to model-theoretic and proof-theoretic analysis in recent years. We will consider models for possibility and necessity in the next section and attend briefly to the issue of proofs for modality here. What could we do to *prove* $\Box A$, the claim that $A$ is necessary? What could we do to infer something *from* $\Box A$. One option is to take our inspiration from the universal quantifier and take these to be our rules:

$$
\begin{array}{cc}
\begin{array}{c} X \\ \Pi \\ \dfrac{A}{\Box A}\ \Box I \end{array}
&
\dfrac{\Box A}{A}\ \Box E
\end{array}
$$

We have the *proviso* on $\Box I$: Each formula in $X$ must start with a $\Box$. The elimination rule is simple: From $\Box A$ we can infer $A$. Conversely, *if we can infer A from premises that are themselves necessary*, we can also conclude $\Box A$, that $A$ is necessary. For example, we can prove $\Box(p \wedge q)$ from $\Box p$ and $\Box q$, like this:

$$
\dfrac{\dfrac{\dfrac{\Box p}{p}\ \Box E \quad \dfrac{\Box q}{q}\ \Box E}{p \wedge q}\ \wedge I}{\Box(p \wedge q)}\ \Box I
$$

These rules do define a modal logic[28] However, we cannot extend the above-mentioned proof into a proof from $\Box p \wedge \Box q$ to $\Box(p \wedge q)$ in the way you might expect:

$$
\dfrac{\dfrac{\dfrac{\dfrac{\Box p \wedge \Box q}{\Box p}\ \wedge E}{p}\ \Box E \quad \dfrac{\dfrac{\Box p \wedge \Box q}{\Box q}\ \wedge E}{q}\ \Box E}{p \wedge q}\ \wedge I}{\Box(p \wedge q)}\ \Box I
$$

for the application of $\Box I$ in this proof now no longer satisfies the constraint on that rule. The formula $\Box p \wedge \Box q$ does not feature a $\Box$ as its dominant operator.

---

∃x(x is not defined)? No (Feferman, 1995). This motivates a natural variation of the quantifier natural deduction rules, which I discuss elsewhere (Restall, 2019).

[28] It is the modal logic S4. If we allow active assumptions in a $\Box I$ step to start with either a $\Box$ or a $\neg\Box$, this gives rise to S5.

We can construct a proof from this premise to that conclusion but only with detours through other connectives:

$$\cfrac{\cfrac{\cfrac{\cfrac{[\Box p]^1}{p}\,\Box E \quad \cfrac{[\Box q]^2}{q}\,\Box E}{p \wedge q}\,\wedge I}{\cfrac{\Box(p \wedge q)}{\Box p \to \Box(p \wedge q)}\,\to I^1 \quad \cfrac{\cfrac{\Box p \wedge \Box q}{\Box p}\,\wedge E}{}\to E}{\cfrac{\Box(p \wedge q)}{\Box q \to \Box(p \wedge q)}\,\to I^2 \qquad \cfrac{\Box p \wedge \Box q}{\Box q}\,\wedge E}{\Box(p \wedge q)}\,\to E$$

So rules like these are not particularly pleasing, and in general, natural deduction and sequent calculus systems for modal logics are difficult to work with.

One alternative proof-theoretic approach is inspired by the treatment of the quantifiers. Different kinds of logical concepts involve different features of our language and how we use that language. Quantifiers trade on terms and substitution, features that play no role in proofs using just the standard propositional connectives. Modal operators trade on something *else*. Let's start with an elimination rule for necessity. It is true that from $\Box A$ we can infer $A$, but this rule far from exhausts the power of the claim of necessity. If we have granted that $A$ is necessary, we can not only infer $A$ 'here' (as it were), we could also infer that it would hold, *were things to be different*. If we structure our dialogue (and our proofs) so that we can allow hypothetical shifts like this, then we could represent the power of the claim to necessity in an appropriately explicit way. Let's represent 'contexts' in our proofs by tagging each line with a label. Lines with the same label are claims made in the same context. If the label changes, we move to a different context, which may be represented in dialogue by words like 'suppose things had gone differently', and the like. The rules for the standard connectives require the context to remain fixed. The rules for the necessity operator allow for contexts to shift. They look remarkably similar to the quantifiers, but instead of quantifying over *objects*, we generalise across *contexts* in dialogue.[29]

$$\begin{array}{c} X \\ \Pi \\ \cfrac{A \cdot i}{\Box A \cdot j}\,\Box I \qquad \cfrac{\Box A \cdot i}{A \cdot j}\,\Box E \end{array}$$

---

[29]  See Read (2008, 2015) for more on proof systems of this form.

Here, in $\Box E$, we allow the context index to shift *arbitrarily*, from any index, to any index. In $\Box I$, we *also* allow the context to shift arbitrarily, but only when the index $i$ tagging the formula $A$ does not occur in the assumption set $X$. Using these rules, we can represent the proof from $\Box p \wedge \Box q$ to $\Box(p \wedge q)$ more naturally:

$$\cfrac{\cfrac{\cfrac{\Box p \wedge \Box q \;\cdot\; 1}{\Box p \;\cdot\; 1} \wedge E}{p \;\cdot\; 2} \Box E \qquad \cfrac{\cfrac{\Box p \wedge \Box q \;\cdot\; 1}{\Box q \;\cdot\; 1} \wedge E}{q \;\cdot\; 2} \Box E}{\cfrac{\cfrac{p \wedge q \;\cdot\; 2}{\Box(p \wedge q) \;\cdot\; 1} \Box I}{}\wedge I}$$

This reasoning corresponds to the informal rendering given later in the text, where I have made *explicit* the context shifts as the reasoning proceeds.

> [*C1*] Suppose it's necessary that $p$ and it's necessary that $q$. Here's why it's necessary that $p$ and $q$. Suppose things go differently [*C2*]. Since [*C1*] it's necessary that $p$, we have [*C2*] $p$. Since [*C1*] it's necessary that $q$, we have [*C2*] $q$. So, [*C2*] we have both $p$ and $q$, and since we made no special assumption about how things go [*C2* is arbitrary], we can conclude [*C1*] that it is necessary that $p$ and $q$.

The natural deduction proof is one way to make explicit and precise the kinds of shifts we can do in everyday reasoning. This can be represented in a sequent calculus as well (Poggiolesi, 2008, 2009, 2010; Poggiolesi & Restall, 2012; Restall, 2012).

The similarity to the rules for quantifiers is striking, and it has led some to ask the question: are modal operators *really* just quantifiers? If we think of the context markers as representing *items*, then it is natural to think of them as *worlds*, at which claims are true or false. If we were to model necessity as a quantifier over worlds, then we could save on rules for logical vocabulary. One consequence of this view is that the semantic structure of claims becomes more complex. The claim of the form 'Socrates is talking', which was formerly a predication $Ts$, and which might be asserted or denied in different contexts, becomes a binary predication, $Tsw$ (Socrates is talking in world $w$), which then has the appropriate form over which the quantifier can operate. Is this the correct form to analyse our language and the structure of our claims about the world? That's one point of difference to be explored, concerning the scope and significance of modal vocabulary.

Notice that this question is related to, but is distinct from, the question of the *ontology* of possible worlds. You could reject the notion that possible worlds are *real existences* and still think that modal operators are disguised quantifiers that range over worlds. (You just need to give a story about quantifiers over worlds

that works for the metaphysically thin understanding of worlds that you have.)
More on this in the next section where we discuss possible worlds semantics,
so it is to this that we now turn.

## 3 Models

*Proofs* were our focus in the previous section. A proof is a certificate for the
*validity* of an argument. If I have a proof from premises to a conclusion, that cer-
tifies that the argument from the premises to the conclusion is *valid*. Models –
our focus for this section – help us view the other side of the coin. If you want
a certificate for the *invalidity* of an argument, you want a counterexample. A
counterexample to an argument is a model, which shows how to satisfy the
premises without at the same time satisfying the conclusion.

So, if we start with this role of models as counterexamples to arguments,
we see that at the very least, we want a model to specify when it *satisfies* a
formula (let's write this '$m \Vdash A$') and when it *doesn't* (let's write this '$m \nVdash A$').
Then, we will say that the model $m$ is a counterexample to the argument from
the premises $X$ to the conclusion $A$ just when $m \Vdash B$ for each $B \in X$, and
$m \nVdash A$.

### 3.1 Two Truth Values

From here it is a very short jump to the idea of classical *two-valued models*,
which give rise to what we call 'truth tables'. Select two items (most commonly
'1' and '0') to represent truth and falsity, and for every atomic formula, we
specify the truth status of the formula by fiat. A *model* is specified by a choice
of truth value for each atomic formula. A model $m$ is a function assigning a
truth value to each atomic formula. $m(p) = 1$ or 0, for each atom $p$. Then, given
this function assigning values to atoms, we can specify how the model assigns
values to the other propositional formulas in a natural way:

| $A$ | $B$ | $\perp$ | $\neg A$ | $A \wedge B$ | $A \vee B$ | $A \rightarrow B$ |
|---|---|---|---|---|---|---|
| 0 | 0 | 0 | 1 | 0 | 0 | 1 |
| 0 | 1 | 0 | 1 | 0 | 1 | 1 |
| 1 | 0 | 0 | 0 | 0 | 1 | 0 |
| 1 | 1 | 0 | 0 | 1 | 1 | 1 |

The table indicates how the logical constants $\perp$, $\neg$, $\wedge$, $\vee$ and $\rightarrow$ interact with
two-valued models. The formula $\perp$ receives the value 0 in every model. In any
model $m$, $m(\neg A)$ is the opposite value to $m(A)$. $m(A \wedge B) = 1$ when and only
when $m(A) = 1$ and $m(B) = 1$ and so on.

So, a model $m$ assigns values 1 or 0 to every formula. We will say that a model $m$ *verifies* a formula $A$ ($m \Vdash A$) iff $m(A) = 1$, and so, $m \nVdash A$ iff $m(A) \neq 1$, which means here that $m(A) = 0$. The result is a classical two-valued logic. We say that $X \vDash_{TV} A$ if and only if there is no model $m$ that is a counterexample to the argument $X \succ A$.

So, now we have models and proofs as two different analyses of validity. The *soundness* theorem states that if we ever have a proof from $X$ to $A$, then indeed $X \vDash A$. The *completeness* theorem is its converse, and the most straightforward way to demonstrate completeness is by proving the converse: if $X \nvDash A$ then we construct a model as a counterexample to the argument from $X$ to $A$.[30]

How does this compare to the discussion of the last section? Let's consider first the treatment of the logical connectives. The meaning rules for the connectives are given in terms of *truth conditions*, rather than introduction and elimination rules. They are similar: very similar. There is a very short step from $\wedge I$ to the left-to-right direction of the biconditional between $m(A) = 1$ and $m(B) = 1$ and $m(A \wedge B) = 1$. However, one is stated in terms of truth-value assignments and the other in terms of *inference*. The same parallel but difference holds for the rules for the other connectives. We can see the similarity if we either understand the inference rules as concerning *truth* (read $\wedge I$ with a *sotto voce* 'is true' after each claim, rather than merely *asserting* them), or conversely, if you think of the values 1 and 0 as ways of specifying *ideal positions* a reasoner might take, concerning claims. There is clearly an interpretive distinction between how we understand proofs and models (to be explored in the next section) but the formal results concerning soundness and completeness should reassure us that connections can be drawn between these two approaches.

The second differerence between the two presentations of the rules is that the ambient background context in one case is the two-valued assignment system that assigns one of two values to each formula, and in the other, the background assumptions about proofs and how they can be composed. In the next section we will explore what we might say about the connections between these two understandings of the background context. For now, we will focus on what insight we can gain concerning the paradoxes, when we pay attention to *models*.

Let's start with the treatment of vague language and the *sorites paradox*. If we look at the sorites paradoxical argument, introduced in Section 1, then we can see that when we analyse the sorites argument (8, see page 7),

(8′)　$R_1$

　　　$R_1 \rightarrow R_2$

---

$R_2 \rightarrow R_3$

$\vdots$

$R_{9\ 999} \rightarrow R_{10\ 000}$

Therefore, $R_{10\ 000}$.

it has no counterexample. If $m(R_1) = 1$ and $m(R_i \rightarrow R_{i+1}) = 1$ for each $i$, then, of necessity, $m(R_{10\ 000}) = 1$ too. If we had a model in which $m(R_1) = 1$ and $m(R_{10\ 000}) \neq 1$ then, of necessity, there would be some value of $i$ where $m(R_i) = 1$ and $m(R_{i+1}) = 0$. There would be some spot along the strip that was red and the next spot along – visually indistinguishable from it – would *not* be red. Clearly there is *something* defective about such a model, given that we have no way of isolating such a spot along the strip. At the very least, it overgenerates precision, where the phenomena at hand does not have such precision to give.

So, a response to this argument is to say that to think of any one model like this as representing 'how things *really* are' goes too far. Of course, some spots along the strip (1, 2 and some more along to the left) are clearly red, and others along the right end are clearly not red, but there is an undetermined middle, where we can go either way. There is no one model that represents how things *are*, but there is a *range* of valuations that all represent equally good sharpenings of our unsharp concepts. Given some non-empty *set s* of two-valued evaluations – a *super*valuation – we will say that a sentence is *super*-true iff it is true according to all of them, and it is *super*-false iff it is false according to all of them, and it is *unsettled* otherwise. (So, where $s$ is a set of valuations, we'll say that $s \Vdash^+ A$ iff $m \Vdash A$ for every $m \in s$, and $s \Vdash^- A$ iff $m \nVdash A$ for every $m \in s$.) The unsettled sentences are those that are true in some valuations in the supervaluation and false in others. On this view, it makes sense to say that $R_1$ is super-true and $R_{10\ 000}$ is super-false, and that the transition premises $R_i \rightarrow R_{i+1}$ are *almost* but *not quite* super-true. Each such premise is true in almost all of the valuations, but if one acceptable way to draw the line between red and nonred falls between $i$ and $i + 1$, then the conditional will be false in that valuation, and true in all of the valuations that cut the line elsewhere. This goes some way to diagnose the paradox. Even though it is not the case in any valuation that the premises are all true and the conclusion false, and it is also not the case that the premises are *super*-true and the conclusion is not super-true, the premises are all at least *almost* super-true and the conclusion is super-false. This is one way to utilise the tools of valuations to diagnose the paradox of vagueness.

One virtue of this approach is that validity as defined as preservation of super-truth, is very close to the validity relation we have already seen. If we define supervaluational validity as preservation of super-truth like this – $X \vDash_{SV} A$ iff for each supervaluation $s$, where $s \Vdash^{+} B$ for each $B \in X$, then $s \Vdash^{+} A$ too – then the relation $\vDash_{SV}$ simply is $\vDash_{TV}$.

Here is why: If $X \nvDash_{TV} A$ then we have some model $m$ where $m \Vdash B$ for each $B \in X$ and $m \nVdash A$. But then $\{m\} \Vdash^{+} B$ for each $B \in X$ and $\{m\} \nVdash^{+} A$, so $X \nvDash_{SV} A$ too. On the other hand, if $X \nvDash_{SV} A$, we have some supervaluation counterexample $s$, where $s$ verifies every member of $X$ but fails to verify $A$. Since $s \nVdash^{+} A$, we have $m \nVdash A$ for some $m \in s$, and since $m \in s$, $m$ verifies every member of $X$, so this $m$ is also a two-valued counterexample to $X \succ A$.

However, if we extend our arguments to full sequents of the form $X \succ Y$, where a counterexample to such a sequent is a model that verifies each member of $X$ and fails to verify each member of $Y$, then in this wider setting, $\vDash_{TV}$ and $\vDash_{SV}$ diverge. We have $\vDash_{TV} p, \neg p$, since there are no two-valued valuations that fail to verify both $p$ and $\neg p$. However, $\nvDash_{SV} p, \neg p$. Any supervaluation with some valuations that verify $p$ and some that verify $\neg p$ will be a counterexample. Similarly, we have $A \vee B \vDash_{TV} A, B$, while $A \vee B \nvDash_{SV} A, B$. Supervaluational validity, comes apart from standard two-valued validity in this wider setting.

So, this view comes at costs that require some kind of response. For one thing, although neither $R_i$ nor $\neg R_i$ is super-true for intermediate cases, the disjunction $R_i \vee \neg R_i$ remains super-true. So, too is the existential claim 'there is a sharp borderline between red and non-red' which is plausibly true in every valuation, but of course, the point of this analysis is that there is no sharp borderline.

Before turning to other approaches to truth values and vagueness, let's consider the interaction between two-valued validity and the semantic paradoxes. If we are committed to understand validity as $\vDash_{TV}$ or $\vDash_{SV}$, then the liar paradoxical and Curry paradoxical arguments are impeccable, except for the steps involving the truth and membership predicates.

For this reason, defenders of a robust theory of truth and class membership, satisfying *TI*/*TE* and $\in$*I*/$\in$*E* in their full generality seek some account of validity other than that given by classical two-valued models. It is not hard to see where you might first look: perhaps there are more truth values than the two supplied by our truth tables. If we assign the liar sentence a truth value other than 1 and 0, then we may see where the argument breaks down. For this, we must explore more truth values.

## 3.2 Beyond Two Truth Values

So, let's consider another way to respond to both the semantic paradoxes and the vagueness in our continuously shading strip. We agree with the supervaluationist that some of the claims $R_i$ are simply *true*, others are simply *false*, but some, in the indeterminate middle, are in a *gap* between truth and falsity. Instead of modelling this with a range of two-valued evaluations, another approach asks us to expand each *single* valuation, by allowing for formulas to take an inter-mediate value – *n*. Having an extra semantic value to give to sentences like the liar would also allow us to give a different response to the semantic paradoxes, so this seems like an approach worth exploring. Once we move from two val-ues to more than two values, we need to expand our valuation conditions. An appealing approach is to take our truth conditions, and to drop the exclusivity condition for valuations, and we have these clauses, governing *three*-valued valuations:

- $m(A \wedge B) = 1$ iff $m(A) = 1$ and $m(B) = 1$,
  $m(A \wedge B) = 0$ iff $m(A) = 0$ or $m(B) = 0$.

- $m(A \vee B) = 1$ iff $m(A) = 1$ or $m(B) = 1$,
  $m(A \vee B) = 0$ iff $m(A) = 0$ and $m(B) = 0$.

- $m(A \rightarrow B) = 1$ iff $m(A) = 0$ or $m(B) = 1$,
  $m(A \rightarrow B) = 0$ iff $m(A) = 1$ and $m(B) = 0$.

- $m(\bot) = 0$.

Here, if the atoms receive the values 0 or 1, the models are traditional two-valued valuations, and truth and falsity acts as expected. If we allow an atom to receive a third value – *n*, say – then some complex formulas also receive the value *n*, in ways governed by these clauses. If $m(p) = n$ then $m(\neg p) = n$ and $m(p \vee \neg p) = m(p \wedge \neg p) = n$ too. Three-valued valuations of this kind differ from two-valued logic and supervaluations in many ways, but in some ways, they are rather familiar.[31]

With these three-valued valuations at hand, the task of defining what it is for a model to provide a counterexample to an argument becomes more compli-cated. Each valuation *m* provides a *tripartite* verdict for formulas, rather than a bipartite one, and so, we have many more options to consider for when an argu-ment is valid. Different options will give different analyses of the paradoxes. Let's start with the first option: validity in Kleene's (strong) three-valued logic is defined by setting $X \vDash_{K3} A$ iff whenever $m(B) = 1$ for each $B \in X$, then $m(A) = 1$ too (Kleene, 1950). This understanding of validity takes *truth* to consist in having the value 1, and validity to be preservation of truth. On this

---

[31]  For example, $m(\neg\neg A) = m(A)$ for each $A$, $m(\neg(A \vee B)) = m(\neg A \wedge \neg B)$, $m(\neg(A \wedge B)) = m(\neg A \vee \neg B)$, $m(A \rightarrow B) = m(\neg A \vee B)$, and many other familiar equivalences hold.

view, it is possible for a formula and its negation to both fail to be *true* (when its value is *n*), and so, it hews closely to the analysis of vagueness given by supervaluations. The difference with suprevaluations is that the tripartite distinction between truth, falsity (which we can define as truth of the negation – *A* is false iff ¬*A* is true) and the *gap* between truth and falsity – is respected by the propositional logical connectives. For these valuations, the status of a complex formula is determined by the status of its components. So, if *A* and ¬*A* are both neither true nor false, so is *A* ∨ ¬*A*. So, on this analysis, if $R_i$ is a statement saying that a given borderline item on the strip is red, then $R_i ∨ ¬R_i$ is also a borderline statement. The approach to the *logic* of the connectives is now highly non-classical, and the divergence from classical logic is much greater than for supervaluation semantics.

The same can be said for the semantic paradoxes. If we consider the proofs for the liar paradox or Curry's paradox, we see that in this proof a crucial step fails to be *K*3-valid. The inference step ¬*I* does not meet the standards of *K*3-validity in the following way. We may indeed have $X, A ⊨_{K3} ⊥$, in that there may be no valuation that makes each member of *X*, and *A* have the value 1. This does not mean, however, that we have $X ⊨_{K3} ¬A$. For there may well be a model where each member of *X* is true and *A* is assigned *n*, and so, therefore, is ¬*A*. On the *K*3 approach, the liar paradoxical reasoning breaks down. It is consistent to assign the liar sentence the value *n*, in which case it has the same value as its negation. It seems that this simple modification of two-valued valuations gives insight into the paradoxical arguments.

≻ ≺

Let's return to the interpretation of these three-valued tables. Instead of interpreting *n* in the way governed by K3-validity, we could instead recover a validity notion by taking an argument to have a counterexample when there is some valuation where the conclusion is assigned the value 0 and the premises are each assigned a value *other than* 0. This is equally a generalisation of the classical two-valued account to this new setting, and on this perspective, *A* ∨ ¬*A* is now valid, but we do not have $A ∧ ¬A ≻ ⊥$. An assignment giving *A* the value *n* now (weakly) satisfies *A* ∧ ¬*A*, in the sense that this formula is never assigned the value 0, and so, contradictions are not explosive. We have ways to make them non-false. On this, *LP*-understanding of validity, the liar-paradoxical argument also breaks down, not at the ¬*I* step, but rather at ¬*E*, since $A, ¬A ⊭_{LP} ⊥$. Here, the argument fails since there are valuations that at least weakly satisfy *A* and ¬*A*, and so, these formulas are not jointly *LP*-unsatisfiable. Here, the liar paradox does not fall into a truth-value *gap*. It is rather in the *glut*, which may be understood as an overlap between truth and falsity (Priest, 1979).

So, we have two different interpretations of the one class of valuations: one, in which a formula assigned the value $n$ is, in some sense, neither true nor false, (here, a valuation that assigns the premises 1 and the conclusion $n$ is a counterexample), and the other, in which a formula assigned the value $n$ is, in some sense, both true and false, (here, a valuation assigning the premises $n$ and the conclusion 0 is a counterexample). Truth-value gaps and truth-value gluts, modelled in just this manner, have proved to provide a rich vein of logical tools and techniques, not only in the modelling of the paradoxes, but also in accounts of content, information carried by inconsistent or incomplete databases and so on (Belnap, 1977a; Blamey, 1986; Dunn, 2000).

Instead of pursuing the different applications of gaps and gluts, we will pause to consider one of the most elegant formal properties of such models. We have seen that the trivialising proofs fail to be $K3$ and $LP$ valid. This should give us some hope that expanding our scope to these models gives us some way of modelling semantic concepts like a robust truth predicate without collapse into triviality. At least *this* proof of triviality fails. But what if there are others? Is there some way to show that there is no proof of triviality, using logically valid notions (whether $K3$ or $LP$) and the truth rules? It turns out that there is an ingenious argument, due independently to Brady (1971), Gilmore (1974), Martin and Woodruff (1975) and Kripke (1975), that shows that no trivialising argument like this is possible, given the three-valued valuations of this kind. We can construct a *model* in which $T^\ulcorner A \urcorner$ is always assigned the same value as $A$, even in the presence of fixed point sentences such as $\lambda$.

The details are subtle, but it is not too difficult to sketch the key ideas of the proof. The most important insight is that we can think of our semantic values, 1, $n$ and 0 as 'ordered' with $n \sqsubset 1$ and $n \sqsubset 0$, but with 0 and 1 incomparable by $\sqsubset$. The key idea is that $n$ is *less specific* as a value than either 0 or 1. Think of something assigned the value $n$ as nascently containing the possibility of 'resolving' into 0 or into 1. (Whether this is a gap being supplied a value where there was none, or a glut being specified into one of the cases makes no difference. It works either way.) The elegant fact in the language of our connectives is that each connective *respects* the order in the following way. If we extend the order to *valuations* like this: $m_1 \sqsubseteq m_2$ iff $m_1(p) \sqsubseteq m_2(p)$ for each atom $p$ (so $m_2$ differs from $m_1$ only by resolving some atoms that were valued $n$ by $m_1$ to be valued 1 or 0 by $m_2$, but it never changes a 1 to a 0 or *vice versa*), then this fact is extends to the entire language: $m_1(A) \sqsubseteq m_2(A)$ for *every* formula $A$. We can verify this fact by examining the evaluation clauses for the connectives, and reasoning as follows. Suppose $m_1(A) \sqsubseteq m_2(A)$. Then $m_1(\neg A) \sqsubseteq m_2(\neg A)$, since if $m_1(\neg A) = 1$ then $m_1(A) = 0$ and, since $m_1(A) \sqsubseteq m_2(A)$, $m_2(A) = 0$, and so $m_2(\neg A) = 1$ too. Similarly, if $m_1(\neg A) = 0$ then $m_1(A) = 1$ and, since $m_1(A) \sqsubseteq m_2(A)$, $m_2(A) = 1$, so $m_2(\neg A) = 0$ too. The same goes for all the connectives we have discussed. They are 'monotonic' with respect to this ordering of semantic values.

This means we can construct models for semantic notions like the truth predicate that validate the *TI/E* rules. In particular, this construction makes models for the truth predicate that ensure that $m(T^\ulcorner A^\urcorner) = m(A)$ for each formula $A$. You might think that this would be straightforward: simply impose this clause for evaluating truth claims, in the same way that we gave clauses for each of the connectives. However, fixed points and self-referential sentences like $\lambda$ means that this procedure will not, in general, work. We need to assign a value to $Tt$ for each term $t$, whether this is a quotation term or not. The term $\lambda$ is given in such a way that $\lambda = \ulcorner \neg T\lambda \urcorner$, that is, the term $\lambda$ and the quotation term $\ulcorner \neg T\lambda \urcorner$ denote the same object in our model. If we attempt to use the simple-minded clause for interpreting $T$ sentences in our model, we notice that $T\lambda$ should get the same value as $T^\ulcorner \neg T\lambda \urcorner$, which (by that clause) should get the same value as $\neg T\lambda$. We can see, given our truth tables, that $n$ is the only value that will suffice, but the reasoning we used to reach to this conclusion should give us pause: the clause for evaluating $T$-sentences did not send us from complex formulas to simpler formulas. In this case, we were sent from $T\lambda$ to $\neg T\lambda$, which is more complex than $T\lambda$.

The situation is more stark if we consider a 'truth-teller' sentence $\tau$, which is given by setting $\tau = \ulcorner T\tau \urcorner$. (In everyday English, it is the sentence 'this very sentence is true'.) Now, if we attempt to evaluate $T\tau$, we have to ask first for the value of $T\tau$. This is a very tight loop, and it gets us nowhere informative. The value of 'this sentence is true', on this account, is whatever the value of 'this sentence is true' happens to be. The simple-minded evaluation conditions for $T$-formulas are not reductive in the way that the conditions for our connectives are. To find models, we need to do something more sophisticated, and this is where the ordering relation $\sqsubseteq$ enters the picture.

We define our model $m_*$ like this: start with a model $m_0$ that interprets the entire language in whatever way we please, except that each $T$-sentence has the value $n$. This defines $m_0$. Now, given *any* model $m_i$ so far defined, we define the *next* model in this process, $m_{i+1}$ by assigning its atomic sentences in just the same way as $m_i$ does, *except* for the $T$ sentences. Here, we assign $T^\ulcorner A^\urcorner$ the same value that the model $m_i$ assigns to the sentence $A$. The crucial insight of this process is that for every sentence at all, $m_i(A) \sqsubseteq m_{i+1}(A)$. The values assigned to sentences in the $m_{i+1}$ are more refined those assigned in $m_i$, as some formulas previously given the value $n$ resolve into the values 1 or 0, but none flip from 1 to 0 or from 0 to 1. This is proved by an inductive argument on the complexity of the formulas, together with the fact that this preservation fact holds for all previous models in the series. (We will not go through the details here: they are discussed at length in the references mentioned earlier.)

This process goes on, *ad infinitum*. Indeed, each model $m_0, m_1, \ldots, m_n, \ldots$, where $n \in \omega$, is more refined than the previous model, and at no point in this sequence does refinement end. So, we continue to $\omega$ and beyond, defining $m_\omega$ to be the natural *limit* of the process, where $m_\omega(T^\ulcorner A^\urcorner) = 1 \; [= 0]$ iff $m_n(T^\ulcorner A^\urcorner) = 1 \; [= 0]$ for some earlier model $m_n$. Continuing, we can define $m_\kappa$ for any ordinal $\kappa$, and now we utilise the fact that the process is monotonic to tell us that the process *must* grind to a halt. If there are strictly more ordinals than there are sentences in our original language (as there are, if the language is bounded by *some* ordinal), then the sets of formulas assigned 1 (and those assigned 0) must eventually reach their fill, and once $m_\kappa = m_{\kappa+1}$, then the process stops completely, and this model is a fixed point, for in *this* model, $m_\kappa(T^\ulcorner A^\urcorner) = m_{\kappa+1}(T^\ulcorner A^\urcorner) = m_\kappa(A)$, for each and every formula $A$.

So, we have seen that there indeed *is* a model with fixed points for the truth predicate. This shows us that we can find a semantic evaluation for our language that strongly identifies $T^\ulcorner A^\urcorner$ and $A$, and so, we have a model that shows that the account of truth does not prove hopelessly trivial.

Notice that this construction is independent of our choice of *logic*. All that is required is in the models, the connectives be appropriately monotonic with respect to the ordering $\sqsubseteq$. There is nothing in this construction about the appropriate notion of *counterexample* that is used. We have, simultaneously, the non-triviality result for the logics *K3* and *LP*, since we can *add* to the brute fact of having this model, the two different understandings of how a model is to be interpreted. Viewing things from the vantage point of *K3*, we have a model in which the liar is neither true nor false (since its value is *n*). As far as *LP* is concerned, we have constructed a model in which the liar is both true and false. The same tools can be used to build quite different theories.

The order $\sqsubseteq$ – and its use in this model construction – imposes a significant constraint on our logical vocabulary. Not every truth table is monotonic with respect to $\sqsubseteq$. Consider the table for the conditional. Defenders of truth-value gaps and truth-value gluts each have reason to take this table to be less than ideal as a model for the conditional. Consider first the *K3*-partisan, the so-called 'conditional' fails to be reflexive. If $m(p) = n$ then $m(p \rightarrow p) = n$, and so $\nvDash_{K3} p \rightarrow p$. Yet, even given truth-value gaps there is a sense in which *if* the liar is true, then the liar is true. It is just that this sense of 'if' cannot be encoded by the conditional of *K3*.

Similarly, in *LP*, the conditional '$\rightarrow$' fails to be *detachable*, in that we have counterexamples to *modus ponens*. Models $m$ where $m(p) = n$ and $m(q) = 0$ ensure $p, p \rightarrow q \nvDash_{LP} q$.

These failures are not incidental. There is no good way to repair the truth tables while keeping (a) the *K3* or *LP* notions of counterexamples, (b) keeping the 'classical' behaviour of the truth table of the conditional for the inputs 0 and 1, and (c) preserving monotonicity over $\sqsubseteq$. Since $m(1 \rightarrow 0) = 0$ and $m(1 \rightarrow 1) = 1$ (by the Boolean condition) we must have $m(1 \rightarrow n) = n$, and so, $m(n \rightarrow n) = n$ (by monotonicity). Hence, we have a *K3*-counterexample to $\succ p \rightarrow p$. Similarly, since $m(1 \rightarrow 0) = 0$ and $m(0 \rightarrow 0) = 1$ (by the Boolean condition), we must have $m(n \rightarrow 0) = n$ (by monotonicity), and hence, we have an *LP*-counterexample to $p, p \rightarrow q \succ q$. So, there is a strong constraint, given by monotonicity, on the evaluation conditions for conditionals in logics with gaps and with gluts.

The lacuna with conditionals might call into question the enterprise of three-valued interpretations. After all, the conditional is a central notion in logical theorising and we would like to not do without a workable conditional, if at all possible. One way to understand our options is to notice that not only does the conditional fare badly with respect to monotonicity, but so does the notion of counterexample in *K3* and *LP*. We have defined counterexamples in *K3* and *LP* that fail to be monotonic with respect to $\sqsubseteq$, and so, given that $\rightarrow$, with its traditional evaluation table *is* monotonic, we should not be surprised if it would turn out to be ill fitting with the notions of *K3* and *LP* counterexamples.

So, inspired by the clause for $\rightarrow$, we could say that a model $m$ is *properly* a counterexample to the argument from $X$ to $A$ when $m(B) = 1$ for each $B \in X$, and $m(A) = 0$. That's when we have refuted the argument from $X$ to $A$. *This* notion is monotonic, because it will not be revised away as any formulas evaluated $n$ are precisified into either 0 or 1, since each premise is settled as 1 and the conclusion is settled as 0. For *this* notion of (in)validity, once a model refutes an argument, any precisification of that model refutes the argument, too.

$$\succ \prec$$

The picture of validity that results when we take a counterexample in a three-valued model to require that the premises be assigned 1 and conclusions 0, is called *ST-validity*, for Strict/Tolerant validity (Cobreros et al., 2012). On one interpretation, we can think of a formula assigned 1 as being true, when measured to a *strict* standard of evaluation, while a formula assigned 0 fails to be true, even when measured to a *tolerant* standard. The formulas assigned $n$ are those that are not strictly true but not tolerantly untrue. In other words, they are tolerantly true but not strictly true. Since negation flips 1 to 0 and back, we can think of the formulas assigned 0 as strictly *false*. The formulas assigned 1 or $n$ are (at least) *tolerantly* true, while the formluas assigned $n$ or 0 are (at least) *tolerantly* false. For a counterexample, on this picture, we want a *clear* counterexample: an assignment according to which the premises are strictly true and the conclusion is strictly false. For an argument to be valid, whenever the premises are *strictly* true, the conclusion is at least *tolerantly* true. Hence, ST-validity.

This picture has some pleasing properties. On this view of counterexamples, both reflexivity ($\succ A \rightarrow A$) and *modus ponens* ($A, A \rightarrow B \succ B$) remain *valid*, for the everyday material conditional. $A \rightarrow A$ never has the value 0 in any model, so it has no counterexample. And, as happens classically, in no model can we assign $A$ and $A \rightarrow B$ the value 1 while assigning $B$ the value 0. In fact *every* classically valid argument $X \succ A$ is valid, under *ST* semantics. If we had some $m$ where $m(X) = 1$ and $m(A) = 0$ then simply refine $m$ into a classical evaluation $m'$ assigning 1 or 0 to each atom, and by monotonicity $m'(X) = 1$ and $m'(A) = 0$, and this remains a *TV* counterexample to our argument. This is a way to preserve *all* of the validities of classical logic, while keeping fixed points for the truth predicate.

But ... isn't that *impossible*? Don't we have a proof to a contradiction using the fixed point for truth and classical principles? Isn't our search for a logic with the means to allow for fixed points motivated by having to move away from strong systems like classical logic or intuitionistic logic, for weaker accounts of proofs – or richer accounts of models – that block one or other of the steps used in the paradoxical derivations. Have we ended up in some bizarre world where we can have our cake and eat it too? Have we missed something along the way? Could we have avoided all the hard work in the last section, and kept all of classical logic and kept safe from the paradoxes?

The answer is – like the answer to many important but ambiguous questions – both *yes* and *no*. Explaining why is very useful for gaining a clear perspective on what different things we mean by 'classical logic'. For the first point, I should reassure you: nothing in the previous section needs to be revised. The classical proof (or derivation) of a contradiction from the *TI/E* principles still stands. The proof and the derivation need to be blocked *somewhere*. If all of those proof principles are included in classical logic, then that logic needs to be revised somewhere in order to maintain the *T* principles without collapse into triviality.

What principles are jettisoned in the shift to *ST*-validity? You may have already noticed – CUT. We can have $A \vDash_{ST} B$ and $B \vDash_{ST} C$ without having

$A \vDash_{ST} C.^{32}$ *ST*-validity is a *model-theoretic* perspective on what is involved in jettisoning the structural rule CUT.

In the shift to *ST*-counterexamples, we lose *Cut*, and this is important in our account of the paradoxes. Our Liar derivation tells us that $\lambda = \ulcorner \neg T\lambda \urcorner \succ T\lambda$ and $\lambda = \ulcorner \neg T\lambda \urcorner, T\lambda \succ$. We do *not* conclude from this that $\lambda = \ulcorner \neg T\lambda \urcorner$ must fail. The derivation tells us that — given $\lambda = \ulcorner \neg T\lambda \urcorner$ — $T\lambda$ is not *strictly* true (it cannot be assigned 1) but is *tolerantly* true (it is not assigned 0).

So, all that we have seen in *ST*-validity is consistent with the account of the last section. What is new in this section is the fact that we have made explicit that despite the absence of *Cut* we can still derive every classically valid sequent. The rule we have jettisoned, *Cut*, is not required for the derivation of any sequent in the propositional vocabulary. We have sketched the proof that *Cut* is eliminable. There is no requirement to keep *Cut* in order to derive classical sequents such as $A, \neg A \succ$ or $\succ A, \neg A$ or $\neg\neg A \succ A$. So, unlike the case for other accounts of validity, the valid *sequents* include all the classical sequents. We do not need to lose any of classical logic, in *that* sense, to keep the logic safe from paradox.

So, what's the catch?

The catch is, as we have seen in the last section, that *ST*-validity is not transitive, and hence, any account of *proof* for *ST*-validity does not allow for ST-proof to compose, in general. I can construct an *ST* proof from *A* to *B*, you can construct an *ST*-proof from *B* to *C*, but we cannot conclude from this that, when we combine them, we have an *ST*-proof from *A* to *C*. The culprit is, of course, the truth and class membership rules (in the case of semantic paradox). The connective and quantifier rules, in and of themselves, are utterly blameless. On this view, *ST*-proofs are the *normal* proofs, and the issue with the problematic proofs of triviality are that they are not normal, and, furthermore, they do not normalise. It is for this reason that the proofs for $\succ T\lambda$ and $T\lambda \succ$ do not compose. Is this a workable theory of proof and of consequence? There is more to be done to see whether we can live within these constraints.

$$\succ \prec$$

One way to soften the blow concerning the failure of composition of proofs is to notice that ST-validity can compose in a more limited sense, with *other* notions of validity. Notice that K3-validity is, to use the '*ST*' vocabulary, SS-validity

---

[32] For one example, suppose *B* receives the value *n* on *every* evaluation, while *A* is 1 and *C* is 0.

(in which truth, constrained *strictly*, is preserved). Similarly, LP-validity is TT-validity, for which *tolerantly* constrained truth is preserved. We immediately have the following *limited* transitivity facts:

- If $X \vDash_{K3} A$ and $Y, A \vDash_{ST} Z$ then $X, Y \vDash_{ST} Z$,
- If $X \vDash_{ST} B, Y$ and $B \vDash_{LP} Z$ then $X \vDash_{ST} Y, Z$.

Any *ST*-validity can be extended *upstream*, using the stricter *K3* standards, and can be extended *downstream*, using the stricter *LP* standards. *ST*-validity in and of itself is not *self*-extending, unlike *LP*- or *K3*-validity, but it does allow for its extension in both directions by means of these consequence relations. This is a case where logical pluralism – attention to more than one consequence relation on the language, operative at the same time, can be of use (Beall & Restall, 2006; Restall, 2014).

There is much more than could be said about *ST*, and its cousin *TS*, which we have not discussed at all, but which corresponds to jettisoning *Id*, as you would expect (French, 2016). In particular, we have not considered *meta*-inferential relations (Barrio et al., 2014, 2019), which become especially important in the land of TS-validity, where there are *no* ground-level valid sequents, in the same way that there are no valid *formulas* in *K3*. These are richly interesting areas that have opened up, from the study of *ST*/*TS* consequence relations.

$$\succ \ \prec$$

There is a sense that *ST*- and *TS*-validity are both different ways to incorporate *aspects* of *K3*- and *LP*-validity into the one system. In one sense, for *ST*- or for *TS*-validity, the semantic value $n$ plays double duty as a truth-value *gap* (when evaluated strictly) and a *glut* (when evaluated tolerantly). So we have a logic that allows for gaps and gluts, in the sense that the (strict) gaps *are* the (tolerant) gluts. On this view, $\succ A \vee \neg A$ is *ST*-valid (because it is never tolerantly deniable) and $A \wedge \neg A \succ$ is *ST*-valid (because $A \wedge \neg A$ is never strictly assertible). However, on the *K3* reading of things, a gap at $A$ leads us to *reject* $A \vee \neg A$, and on the *LP* reading, a glut at $A$ leads us to *accept* $A \wedge \neg A$. In either case, we violate *ST*-constraints. For some, the *ST* understanding for how to have gaps and gluts is altogether too mild, while the *TS* understanding is altogether too drastic, in that *no* seqent is *TS* valid. There is an older way to incorporate both gaps and gluts into a semantic picture, and this is to expand the picture beyond three values, to four: Split our $n$ into two values, $n$ and $b$, with the reading now that $n$ is *neither* and $b$ is *both*.

One way to generate such an understanding of these four 'values' is to revisit the truth conditions seen on page 42, but to discard the assumption that the 'truth' and 'falsity' values assigned to formulas are mutually exhaustive. Instead, let's conceive of the four values 1, 0, $n$ and $b$ as the *sets* {t} (true only), {f} (false only), { } (neither) and {t,f} (both). If we allow an assignment of values to each atomic formula to specify a model $m$, we extend those values to arbitrary formulas in the natural way:

- $t \in m(A \wedge B)$ iff $t \in m(A)$ and $t \in m(B)$,

  $f \in (A \wedge B)$ iff $f \in m(A)$ or $m(B) = 0$.

- $t \in m(A \vee B)$ iff $t \in m(A)$ or $t \in m(B)$,

  $f \in m(A \vee B)$ iff $f \in m(A)$ and $f \in m(B)$.

- $t \in m(A \rightarrow B)$ iff $f \in m(A)$ or $t \in m(B)$,

  $f \in m(A \rightarrow B)$ iff $t \in m(A)$ and $f \in m(B)$.

- $m(\bot) = \{f\}$.

This is a four-valued logic, *FDE* (for *first degree entailment*) (Dunn, 1976; Belnap, 1977a,b). Notice that the reducts to $\{0, n, 1\}$ and $\{0, b, 1\}$ are isomorphic. We have two copies of our three-valued logic, in parallel. If we define *validity* as preservation of $\{1, b\}$, we get both *K3*-validity if we restrict ourselves to $\{0, n, 1\}$-valuations (as preservation of the values $\{1, b\}$ on $\{0, n, 1\}$ amounts to preservation of 1) and *LP*-validity if we restrict ourselves to $\{0, b, 1\}$-valuations. The ordering relation $\sqsubseteq$ (defined by setting $n$ *under* 1 and 0, and $b$ *above* each value), is actually the *subset* relation on our values, understood as subsets of $\{t, f\}$, and each connective is monotone with respect to that ordering. So, model constructions of the kind we sketched earlier, for fixed points, are also possible for four-valued evaluations as well as for the three-valued valuations we've seen. The result is a semantic system that incorporates both truth-value *gaps* and truth-value *gluts*.

Notice that *FDE* consequence is strictly weaker than both *K3* and *LP* consequence, since every *K3* counterexample is an *FDE* counterexample, and also, every *LP* counterexample is (when $n$ is mapped to $b$) also an *FDE* counterexample. So, *FDE* has all of the benefits and all the costs of both these systems. Entailment is transitive and reflexive, so it differs from *ST* and *TS*, and it is natural to ask whether there is a natural analogue of *ST* consequence on the four-valued models of *FDE*. If the aim is to recover all of classical logic, then given that $p \wedge \neg p \succ$ is classically valid, the analogue of *S* here must be $\{1\}$ only, since $p \wedge \neg p$ can be assigned any value other than 1. Similarly, given that $\succ p \vee \neg p$ is classically valid, the analogue of *T* must be $\{1, n, b\}$, since $p \vee \neg p$

can be assigned any value other than 0. To take strict truth to be 1 seems fair enough, but to take tolerant truth to be any among $\{1, n, b\}$ – including $n$ – is to evacuate the distinction between $n$ and $b$ of any significance at all. To adopt an *ST*-style consequence relation on *FDE* models is to look for a logic strictly weaker than classical logic.[33]

≻ ≺

We should turn to the topic of vagueness, to consider how non-bivalent valuations inform our response to the sorites paradox. When we last considered vagueness, we examined *supervaluations*. The approach to vagueness given a rather direct application of three-valued models is not too different than for supervaluations, except that for our three-valued models, we can assign the value $n$ to a borderline statement, and so, the excluded middle statement $p \vee \neg p$ and the contradiction statement $p \wedge \neg p$ is assigned $n$ as well. If we have the *ST* interpretation in focus, then evaluated *strictly*, they both $p \vee \neg p$ and $p \wedge \neg p$ fail to be true, while evaluated *tolerantly*, they are true. Statements like $R_i \vee \neg R_i$ fail to live up to the high standards of strict assertion where $i$ is a borderline case of red. They do count as true, though, if we are tolerant. What goes for the excluded middle alternative statements go also for the contradiction statements $R_i \wedge \neg R_i$. For high standards, they fail. Tolerantly, they succeed.[34]

What goes for conjunctions and disjunctions goes, too, for conditionals. At least some of the transition conditionals $R_i \rightarrow R_{i+1}$ that feature in the sorites argument turn out to be strictly untrue but tolerantly true. So, for the sorites argument, we have many three-valued valuations that make all transition conditionals at least *tolerantly* true, but provided that $R_1$ is assigned 1 and $R_{10\,000}$ is assigned 0, then we cannot have all transition conditionals counting as strictly true.

So, what can we say about the sorites argument, given valuations like this? We have a subtle diagnosis of the paradox. We can grant the pressure in the sorites paradoxical argument, in the following way: The argument is, after all, *ST-valid*. If all the premises are strictly true then the conclusion is at least tolerantly true. There is a sense, too, in which the premises indeed are all *true*. They are all *tolerantly* true. This is not enough, though, for us to derive the conclusion, even to *tolerant* standards. We are not able to guarantee the strict truth of the premises, which is what would be required in order to justify the

---

[33] For a more extended discussion of the connection between *ST*, *TS* and three- and four-valued valuations, see French & Ripley (2018).

[34] This might be surprising, but there is some experimental support for tolerance for contradictions in the case of vagueness (Ripley, 2011).

conclusion. In this way we can explain the appeal of each horn of our trilemma (the validity of the argument – it is *ST*-valid; the truth of the premises – they are tolerantly true; and the falsity of the conclusion – the conclusion is *not* tolerantly true). The tension is alleviated in that tolerant truth is not preserved by *ST*-validity.

There is much more that could be said about these three- and four-valued logical systems and the analysis of logical validity that they afford. However, this section is nearly at an end, and we need to discuss models for quantifiers, for modal operators, and a model-first perspective on rejecting the structural rules of contraction and weakening, so it is to these topics that we will turn.

## 3.3 Worlds: Possible and Impossible

Possible worlds models have proved useful tools in the philosophical logician's toolbox. The key innovation in possible worlds models is evaluating the truth or falsity of a modal statement $\Box A$ or $\Diamond B$ '*here*' in terms of the truth or falsity of $A$ or of $B$ *elsewhere*. In simple possible worlds models we allow for formulas to be evaluated as true or false not just in one interpretation but across a range of them. A model is given by a non-empty *set* $W$ of 'worlds'. The standard connectives are evaluated in the familiar way:

- $w \Vdash \bot$ never,
- $w \Vdash \neg A$ iff $w \nVdash A$,
- $w \Vdash A \wedge B$ iff $w \Vdash A$ and $w \Vdash B$,
- $w \Vdash A \vee B$ iff $w \Vdash A$ or $w \Vdash B$,
- $w \Vdash A \rightarrow B$ iff $w \nVdash A$ or $w \Vdash B$.

So far, the addition of worlds yields nothing new. Each world acts just like a two-valued model.[35] Modal operators make use of worlds. Whether $\Box A$ or $\Diamond B$ is true at one world may depend on the status of $A$ or of $B$ in others. The most simple treatment goes like this:

- $w \Vdash \Box A$ iff $v \Vdash A$ for each $v \in W$,
- $w \Vdash \Diamond A$ iff $v \Vdash A$ for some $v \in W$.

If we define validity as usual, setting $X \vDash A$ iff for each model, and each world $w$ in that model, if $w$ satisfies each member of $X$ it also satisfies $A$, then the result is a simple semantics, sufficient for the modal logic s5, mentioned in the previous section.

---

[35] We could extend the picture to allow for three- or four-valued valuations, of course, but we keep things simple for the moment.

For these models, $\neg\Box A \succ \Box\neg\Box A$ is valid. If $w \Vdash \neg\Box A$ then $w \nVdash \Box A$ and so, there is some $v \in W$ where $v \nVdash A$. It follows that $w \Vdash \Box\neg\Box A$, since for *any* $x \in W$, $x \Vdash \neg\Box A$, since $v \nVdash A$.

However, there is no S4 proof from $\neg\Box A$ to $\Box\neg\Box A$, so if we want our models to correspond to stricter S4 proofs, we need to allow for more models, to provide more counterexamples. The key idea is the notion of *relative* necessity. In these S5 models, what is necessary or not is *absolute*, not varying from world to world. In models for S4, we allow what is not necessary to vary. Sometimes, what is not necessary is *necessarily* not necessary – but not always. So, if we add an *accessibility relation* to our models, we can distinguish from among the overall collection of worlds, those worlds that are possible from the point of view of a given world $w$. We write '$wRv$' to indicate that, in to our model, from world $w$, world $v$ counts as possible. We then revise our truth conditions as follows:

- $w \Vdash \Box A$ iff $v \Vdash A$ for each $v \in W$ where $wRv$,
- $w \Vdash \Diamond A$ iff $v \Vdash A$ for some $v \in W$ where $wRv$.

The unrelativised conditions produced more than S4 while the relativised truth conditions produce less. If we leave things as they stand, we have models with worlds $w$ where $w \Vdash \Box p$ but $w \nVdash p$ (if $wRw$ fails). Similarly, we can have $w \Vdash \Box p$ but $w \nVdash \Box\Box p$ (if we have $w, v, x$ where $wRv$ and $vRx$ but not $wRx$). However, it is well known that if we impose the constraint that $R$ is transitive (so, whatever world is accessible to an accessible world is itself accessible) and reflexive (what holds is possible) then we get exactly S4.[36]

Possible worlds semantics in this way has proved very useful as a modelling tool for a wide range of modal logics beyond S4 and S5. Instead of focusing on the range of ways that we can tweak the modal accessibility relation to model this or that other logic,[37] we will look beyond to other ways that worlds play a role in models for logics we have already considered.

Recall the structural rules of WEAKENING and CONTRACTION. Weakening is essential in derivations like these, which conclude in sequents that have come to be known as *fallacies of relevance*.

$$\frac{p}{q \to p} \to I \qquad \frac{\dfrac{\dfrac{[p]^1}{p \to p} \to I^1}{q \to (p \to p)} \to I \qquad q}{p \to p} \to E$$

---

[36] I won't show in detail how we get exactly the logic S4. For that, see (Restall & Standefer, 2022).

[37] There are many good textbooks to introduce this in detail (Chellas, 1980; Gamut, 1991; Hughes & Cresswell, 1996; Blackburn et al., 2001; Beall & van Fraassen, 2003).

In both proofs, we have instances of *vacuous* discharge, where a conditional is introduced, while the antecedent was not active as a premise of the subproof of the conclusion. How might we understand *models*, to provide counterexamples to the sequents $p \succ q \rightarrow p$ and $q \succ p \rightarrow p$?

Modal logics provide room for what is called a *strict* conditional, $\Box(A \rightarrow B)$, where the '$\rightarrow$' in question is the everyday material conditional. Write $\Box(A \rightarrow B)$ as $A \Rightarrow B$. In our simple S5 models we have:

- $w \Vdash A \Rightarrow B$ iff for each world $v$, either $v \nVdash A$ or $v \Vdash B$.

These models provide a simple counterexample to $p \succ q \Rightarrow p$. Take two worlds $w$ and $v$ where $w, v \Vdash q$, while $w \Vdash p$ and $v \nVdash p$. Then it follows that $w \nVdash q \Rightarrow p$ since at $v$, $q$ holds but $p$ doesn't. And this counterexample makes *sense*. A set-up where $p$ holds contingently, while $q$ is necessary will give us circumstances (our $w$) where $p$ holds, but $q \Rightarrow p$ fails: had things gone otherwise (like it does at $v$) where $q$ still holds and $p$ does not. One 'fallacy' is straightforward to refute on this interpretation.

Simple modal models provide no such straightforward counterexample to $q \succ p \Rightarrow p$, since $p \Rightarrow p$ is true at *every* world in these modal models. To find a counterexample to this argument, we must work harder.

$$\succ \prec$$

If we wish to keep this same format for modelling entailment between formulas, we need some point in our model (let's pause before calling this point a 'world' for reasons that will become clear soon) where $p$ holds and where $q \rightarrow q$ fails, where this '$\rightarrow$' is now the new, 'relevant', conditional. One way to achieve this effect – which is in harmony with the motivations behind the conditional given in our proof rules – is to say that a conditional $A \rightarrow B$ holds at a point $x$ if and only if whenever the antecedent $A$ holds at some point $y$, the consequent holds at any point that is *appropriately related* to the pair $\langle x, y \rangle$. In other words, the consequent holds at any points appropriately related to *pairs* of points, one where the conditional holds and the other where the antecedent holds. A conditional is evaluated by *applying* the information at hand (the information giving rise to the conditional) to (perhaps hypothetical) information supporting the antecedent, and if the *result* supports the consequent, the conditional holds.

- $x \Vdash A \rightarrow B$ iff for each $y, z$ where $\langle x, y \rangle Rz$, if $y \Vdash A$ then $z \Vdash B$.

Now, for the fallacies of relevance to have counterexamples, we need $\langle x, y \rangle Rx$ and $\langle x, y \rangle Ry$ to both fail. The result of applying $x$ to $y$ may not return $x$, or return $y$, but may result in *different* information.

(Here is a simple model in which both fallacies of relevance fail in a straightforward manner. Let the set of points in our model be the natural numbers, $\omega$, and set $\langle x,y \rangle Rz$ iff $z = \max(x,y)$ – to *combine* two points, you choose the larger of the two. We can refute the argument from $q$ to $p \rightarrow q$, in a model where $q$ holds at 0 only, while $p$ holds at 1 only, since $0 \Vdash q$, and $1 \Vdash p$ but $\langle 0,1 \rangle R1$, while $1 \nVdash q$. The same model refutes the argument from $p$ to $q \rightarrow q$, since $1 \Vdash p$ while $1 \nVdash q \rightarrow q$, given that $\langle 1,0 \rangle R1$ and $0 \Vdash q$ but $0 \nVdash q$.)

If we wish to stay close to the logical systems that arise out of natural deduction or the sequent calculus, a simple condition on the relation $R$ arises. In our proofs, premises may be freely discharged from any position in a sequent. This corresponds nicely to the fact that the accessibility relation does not distinguish between the *order* in the pair: we have $\langle x,y \rangle Rz$ iff $\langle y,x \rangle Rz$.[38] Similarly, if we impose a kind of *transitivity* condition, to the effect that if $\langle x,y \rangle Rz$ and $\langle z,w \rangle Rv$ then there is some $u$ where $\langle y,w \rangle Ru$ and $\langle x,u \rangle Rv$, then this corresponds to the validity of the prefixing argument:

$$A \rightarrow B \succ (C \rightarrow A) \rightarrow (C \rightarrow B),$$

which has a straightforward proof:

$$
\cfrac{A \rightarrow B \quad \cfrac{\cfrac{[C \rightarrow A]^2 \quad [C]^1}{A} \rightarrow E}{\cfrac{B}{\cfrac{C \rightarrow B}{(C \rightarrow A) \rightarrow (C \rightarrow B)} \rightarrow I^2} \rightarrow I^1}}{} \rightarrow E
$$

Verifying that there is no counterexample to this argument in a model where the relation $R$ satisfies the transitivity condition has the same structure as this natural deduction proof. Consider the reasoning:

> Given a point $x \Vdash A \rightarrow B$, to show $x \Vdash (C \rightarrow A) \rightarrow (C \rightarrow B)$, suppose that $y \Vdash C \rightarrow A$, and that $\langle x,y \rangle Rz$. We want to show, now, that $z \Vdash C \rightarrow B$. To show this, suppose that $w \Vdash C$ and $\langle z,w \rangle Rv$. Now we aim to show that $z \Vdash B$. Here, we appeal to transitivity, to find a point $u$ where $\langle y,w \rangle Ru$ and $\langle x,u \rangle Rv$. Since $\langle y,w \rangle Ru$, $y \Vdash C \rightarrow A$ and $w \Vdash C$, we have $u \Vdash A$, and since $x \Vdash A \rightarrow B$ we have $v \Vdash B$, as desired.

With the transitivity condition at hand, and its converse, we can think of the relation as combining lists of points, rather than pairs. If we compress the conjunction $\langle x,y \rangle Rz$ and $\langle z,w \rangle Rv$ into $\langle \langle x,y \rangle, w \rangle Rv$, and similarly, $\langle x,u \rangle Rv$ and

---

[38] Notice, the example discussed earlier, where $\langle x,y \rangle Rz$ iff $z = \max(x,y)$ on the set $\omega$ satisfies this condition.

$\langle y, w \rangle Ru$ into $\langle x, \langle y, w \rangle \rangle Rz$, then you can see how the transitivity condition and its converse allows us to elide the distinction between $\langle \langle x, y \rangle, w \rangle$ and $\langle x, \langle y, w \rangle \rangle$, and consider the list $\langle x, y, z \rangle$, irrespective of its bracketing.[39] Given this understanding of points and the relation $R$, we can link models and arguments like this: a sequent of the form $P_1, P_2, \ldots, P_n \succ C$ *holds* in a frame if and only if for any points $x_1, \ldots, x_n$ where $\langle x_1, \ldots, x_n \rangle Ry$, if $x_i \Vdash P_i$ for each $i$, then $y \Vdash C$. In other words, to check for a counterexample on a model, we see whether the conclusion of an argument holds at any point appropriately related to a sequence of points at which the premises hold. As with modal logics, different logical systems are given by imposing different conditions on the relation $R$ (Routley & Meyer, 1973; Restall, 2000; Dunn & Restall, 2002). The key feature of these models for our concerns – remember, we are interested in the distinctive role of the structural rules of WEAKENING and CONTRACTION – is that the distinctive relation $R$ plays a role in the behaviour of validity on a model, and does not just involve itself in the interpretation of this or that connective. The argument from $A, B$ to $C$ is valid not just when any point at which $A$ and $B$ both happen to hold is one where $C$ holds – if we were to take *that* as the definition of validity, then weakening would follow immediately – we need $C$ to hold at points that are appropriately related to those where $A$ holds and those where $B$ holds. You need to *combine* the premises in order to get the conclusion.

This perspective on models gives us a natural treatment of CONTRACTION and the significance of rejecting it. For contraction to hold, we require that whenever $\langle x, y_1, \ldots, y_n \rangle Rz$ then $\langle x, x, y_1, \ldots, y_n \rangle Rz$ too. That is, repeated points in our sequence do not introduce *new* accessibility relational constraints. (A special case of this condition is $\langle x, x \rangle Rx$ – which follows from the more general case and the unary relational fact $\langle x \rangle Rx$.) If we reject the CONTRACTION condition, we allow for repetitions in our sequences of points to *count*. Having two points at which $A$ holds might tell us something that having just the one point, did not.[40]

I have sketched here a model system that allows us to faithfully represent the distinctions made in our discipline for proofs.[41] The key question at hand is

---

[39] This is a glimpse at a very general perspective on models for substructural logics. Standefer and I consider models under this guise in more detail, elsewhere (Restall & Standefer, 2021).

[40] The model we discussed earlier, in which weakening fails, where $\langle x_1, \ldots, x_n \rangle Ry$ iff $y = \max(x_1, \ldots, x_n)$, is a model where the contraction rule still holds. Here, repeats do not matter. A simple concrete example of a model in which the contraction condition fails is found by choosing a different relation: $\langle x_1, \ldots, x_n \rangle Ry$ iff $y = x_1 + \cdots + x_n$. Here, repeats clearly *matter*. $\langle 1, 1 \rangle R2$ while we don't have $\langle 1 \rangle R2$.

[41] For more details of this distinctive presentation of the ternary relational semantics for substructural logics, see my paper with Standefer (Restall & Standefer, 2021).

in *this* context, though, what do these models mean?[42] Do models like these help our understanding the distinctions we draw when we accept or reject the structural rules of contraction or weakening?

These questions are specific instances of more general questions, concerning the relationship between *proofs* and *models*, especially when it comes to questions of meaning. So, in the final section, we turn to face these questions head on.

# 4 Connections

In the previous section we introduced both proofs and models for a range of logical systems, and we saw how the different considerations arose out of a concern to model different phenomena, or to provide space for a uniform analysis of the paradoxes of self-reference and of vagueness. In this section, we treat the systems of the previous sections – the proofs and models for these logics – as the materials for philosophical reflection. What does this all *mean*? What can we learn from these proofs and models for different logics?

## 4.1 Soundness and Completeness

As I flagged at the end of the last section, our first stop will be the relationship between proofs and models. We do not have the space to consider proofs and models for every different logical system in our remaining pages, but let's consider, to start, classical logic and its three-valued cousins, *ST*, *K3* and *LP*. Models for these different logics are given in terms of straightforward two-and three-valued evaluations on our language. Proofs for classical logic and *ST* are given in the standard sequent calculus – classical logic, with the full use of *Cut* and *ST* by restraining ourselves from its use. The fact connecting the models and the proofs for Classical logic and *ST* can be stated as follows:

A sequent $X \succ Y$ is *derivable* in classical logic [derivable in ST] iff that sequent has no classical *counterexample* [has no ST counterexample]. In other words, $X \vdash_{CL} Y$ iff $X \vDash_{CL} Y$, and $X \vdash_{ST} Y$ iff $X \vDash_{ST} Y$. This *ST* fact continues to hold in the presence of rules for truth or for class membership.

It is enlightening to consider how we can *prove* this fact. One direction (from $\vdash$ to $\vDash$, from derivability to the absence of a counterexample – the *soundness* half) is achieved by way of an induction on the construction of the derivation. That is, we show that the axiomatic sequent $A \succ A$ is valid (both classically valid,

---

[42] This question has been asked *many* times when it comes to models for relevant logics and their neighbours (Copeland, 1979, 1983; Beall et al., 2012).

and *ST*-valid) and we consider each of the rules one by one, to show that if the premises of the rule are valid, so is the conclusion. Each rule is sound in this sense, in either classical valuations or *ST*-valuations – except for *Cut*, which is merely classically valid, and not *ST*-valid. So, for any classically derivable sequent $X \succ Y$, we have $X \vDash_{CL} Y$. If it is *ST*-derivable, we furthermore have $X \vDash_{ST} Y$.

The other direction, *completeness*, is most easily established by proving its contrapositive: if there is no derivation for some sequent $X \succ Y$ then we have the means to construct a valuation that assigns 1 to each member of $X$ and 0 to each member of $Y$. Let's start with the case where we have $X \nvdash_{ST} Y$. We aim to show that there is a three-valued model $m$ assigning 1 to each member of $X$ and 0 to each member of $Y$. (After showing this, it will be a short step to conclude that if we also have $X \nvdash_{CL} Y$ then there is some two-valued model that is a counterexample.) We can think of $[X : Y]$ as forming a *position*, according to which each member of $X$ is true and each member of $Y$, false. In general, a position is a pair of sets of formulas where there is no derivation of any sequent $X \succ Y$ where the formulas in $X$ are in the left component of the position and the formulas in $Y$ are in the right. We show that $[X : Y]$ may be extended to a *limit* position, a pair $[\mathcal{X} : \mathcal{Y}]$, which is so large that the addition of any formula either to $\mathcal{X}$ or to $\mathcal{Y}$ would result in a pair that is no longer a position. (That is, there would *be* an *ST*-derivation of a sequent $X' \succ Y'$ where $X' \subseteq \mathcal{X}$ and $Y' \subseteq \mathcal{Y}'$.)

How do we find such a limit position? We build it up, step-by-step, by enumerating the formulas in our language in a list, $A_1, A_2, A_3, \dots$. Define $[X_0 : Y_0]$ to be $[X : Y]$. Then, given $[X_n : Y_n]$, define $[X_{n+1} : Y_{n+1}]$ as follows:

$$[X_{n+1} : Y_{n+1}] = \begin{cases} [X_n, A_{n+1} : Y_n] & \text{if } X_{n+1}, A_{n+1} \nvdash_{ST} Y_n, \\ [X_n : A_{n+1}, Y_n] & \text{if } X_{n+1}, A_{n+1} \vdash_{ST} Y_n \text{ and } X_{n+1} \nvdash_{ST} A, Y_n, \\ [X_n : Y_n] & \text{otherwise.} \end{cases}$$

That is, considering each formula, one by one, we add it to the left if the result remains a position, if not, we add it to the right if the result remains a position, and we refrain from adding it to either side only when we could take neither option. The limit of this process, the pair $[\bigcup_{n=0}^{\infty} X_n : \bigcup_{n=0}^{\infty} Y_n] = [\mathcal{X} : \mathcal{Y}]$ is a limit position, by construction. The only formulas left out from either side are those whose addition – on either side – would result in a derivation from the left to the right.

We show, in the next step, that we can assign a valuation assigning 1 to all members of $\mathcal{X}$ and 0 to all members of $\mathcal{Y}$. To do this, we rely on the following facts about *ST*-provability.

- If $X, \neg A \vdash_{ST} Y$ then $X \vdash_{ST} A, Y$.
- If $X \vdash_{ST} \neg A, Y$ then $X, A \vdash_{ST} Y$.
- If $X, A \wedge B \vdash_{ST} Y$ then $X, A, B \vdash_{ST} Y$.
- If $X \vdash_{ST} A \wedge B, Y$ then $X \vdash_{ST} A, Y$ and $X \vdash_{ST} B, Y$.
- If $X, A \vee B \vdash_{ST} Y$ then $X, A \vdash_{ST} Y$ and $X, B \vdash_{ST} Y$.
- If $X \vdash_{ST} A \vee B, Y$ then $X \vdash_{ST} A, B, Y$.
- If $X, A \rightarrow B \vdash_{ST} Y$ then $X, B \vdash_{ST} Y$ and $X \vdash_{ST} A, Y$.
- If $X \vdash_{ST} A \rightarrow B, Y$ then $X, A \vdash_{ST} B, Y$.

These facts are the *converses* of the connective rules in the *ST* sequent calculus. I will not stop to prove each instance, but I will explain the reasoning for the first fact – the others can be proved in the same way. If we have a derivation of $X, \neg A \succ Y$, then trace back every occurrence of $\neg A$ from the conclusion to wherever a linked $\neg A$ first appears. This could be in an identity sequent of the form $\neg A \succ \neg A$, or an instance of a $\neg L$ rule or the $\neg A$ may have been introduced by way of a *weakening* step. (Notice: this reasoning holds whether we use the truth or class membership rules or not, since those rules cannot introduce a negation formula.) In either case, transform our derivation by replacing the occurrence $\neg A$ on the left of the sequent by an instance of $A$ in the right. If the $\neg A$ came by way of an identity sequent, replace it by the sequent $\succ A, \neg A$, given by $\neg R$. If it came by way of a $\neg L$ rule, simply delete that rule occurrence, and leave the un-negated $A$ on the right. If $\neg A$ came by way of weakening, simply weaken in $A$ on the right instead. If we do this uniformly in the derivation, the result is now a derivation of $X \succ A, Y$ instead. The same can be done for *all* our connectives, showing that the connective rules are *invertible*.

This fact has a profound consequence for our limit position $[\mathcal{X} : \mathcal{Y}]$. It acts just like an *ST*-model, where $\mathcal{X}$ collects together everything assigned 1 and $\mathcal{Y}$ contains everything assigned 0. We can show, for example, that $\neg A \in \mathcal{X}$ iff $A \in \mathcal{Y}$ and $\neg A \in \mathcal{Y}$ iff $A \in \mathcal{X}$. Suppose that $\neg A \in \mathcal{X}$, then if $A \notin \mathcal{Y}$ we must have $X' \vdash_{ST} A, Y'$ for some $X' \subseteq \mathcal{X}$ and $Y' \subseteq \mathcal{Y}$ (otherwise we would have added $A$ to the right component when the opportunity arose). So, it follows that $X', \neg A \vdash_{ST} Y'$ and hence, $\neg A \notin \mathcal{X}$, contrary to our hypothesis. Conversely, if $A \in \mathcal{Y}$, that means that we must have $\neg A \in \mathcal{X}$, since if $X', \neg A \vdash_{ST} Y'$ then we must also have $X' \vdash_{ST} A, Y'$ (the fact proved earlier), which contradicts the assumption that $A \in \mathcal{Y}$.

The rest of the conditions for the connectives may be demonstrated in exactly the same way. The upshot is that each limit position $[\mathcal{X} : \mathcal{Y}]$ gives us an *ST*-evaluation $m$, where $m(A) = 1$ iff $A \in \mathcal{X}$ and $m(A) = 0$ iff $A \in \mathcal{Y}$. Completeness for ST follows. If a sequent cannot be derived, then it may be extended into a limit position and that position defines a valuation that is a counterexample to the sequent.

For paradoxical sentences like $T\lambda$, where we can derive both $\succ T\lambda$ and $T\lambda \succ$, the offending sentence is never placed in the left, or in the right, for neither option is available. In any corresponding valuation, it must be assigned $n$, as expected.

What works here works for classical logic too, except in the presence of *Cut*, we know that our limit position $[\mathcal{X} : \mathcal{Y}]$ is a partition of the language – there is no gap between $\mathcal{X}$ and $\mathcal{Y}$ in which formulas (like our $T\lambda$) can escape. It is easy to see why. In the process of constructing our limit position, when consider adding the formula $A_{n+1}$, the only way it could avoid going in either the left or the right of $[X_n : Y_n]$ is if $X_n, A \vdash_{CL} Y_n$ and $X_n \vdash_{CL} A, Y_n$. But by *Cut*, we would have $X_n \vdash_{CL} Y_n$ too, which we don't have, since we are careful to only construct positions. So, having *Cut* in our arsenal means that the positions we construct can satisfy the stronger two-valued, classical constraint.

The argument given here is quite general. It is a comprehensive toolkit for proving the *completeness* theorem for logics like these.[43]

So, we have seen how the soundness and completeness theorems are proved for classical logic and for ST. What can we learn from this about the relationship between proofs and models for these logics? As is most often the case, a pair of purely *formal* mathematical results like the soundness and completeness theorems can be understood and interpreted in more than one way. What are possible ways to interpret these results?

One perspective – and it is the overwhelmingly standard view – is to see models as providing *semantics* for our language, imparting the sentences with meaning, and the proofs provide something else, without meaning, mere *syntax*.[44] This characterisation is implicit in the very vocabulary of 'soundness' and 'completeness' for our theorems. The 'soundness' in the soundness theorem is an evaluation of the proof system, saying it does not overstep the criterion

---

[43] Proving completeness for modal logics, first-order predicate logics, and for logics without weakening or without contraction are more complicated affairs, and we will not go through the detail of those proofs here. For a general discussion of this presentation of the completeness construction, see my 'Truth Values and Proof Theory' (Restall, 2009). For more specifics, see *Logical Methods* (Restall & Standefer, 2022) and also *An Introduction to Substructural Logics* (Restall, 2000).

[44] As just one example, Ted Sider's *Logic for Philosophy* characterises models (truth-value assignments) for propositional logic as 'the semantic approach to logic' whereas proofs are doing something else, something *non-semantic*. 'The definitions of the previous section were inspired by the semantic conception of logical truth and logical consequence. An alternate conception is proof-theoretic' (Sider, 2010, Section 2.5).

established by models. 'Completeness' is similar: it is the proof theory that is complete, when it generates a proof for every valid argument. The very vocabulary presents these as results evaluating a system of proofs for their match (or mismatch) with a system of models.

It would be very strange if essentially *semantic* notions (such as validity) could turn out to be equivalent to purely non-semantic *syntactic* notions (such as provability). The soundness and completeness theorems should cast doubt on the idea that ⊨ is meaning-involving in a way that ⊢ is not. Of course, if the only way to provide *semantics* for an expression is given in terms of a mapping from the language to something like a *model*, then there is a clear sense in which model theory (by its very nature) provides *semantics* (in that narrow sense) in a way that proof theory does not. However, to understand the only way *meaning* arises as coming by way of *representation* is to deprive oneself of other ways to understand semantics. The broad sweep of theories of meaning of the twentieth century also includes non-representationalist *pragmatist* theories of meaning, which take their cue from Wittgenstein's dictum, to the effect that meaning is *use*.[45]

≻ ≺

Given the distinction between inferentialism and representationalism, it is possible also to view the relationship between proof theory and model theory differently, and to approach it from a pragmatist, non-representationalist perspective. As has been argued elsewhere,[46] we can see the *sequent calculus* as presenting semantically significant relationships in its own right, and we can judge the model theory in terms of its match to the theory of proofs. On our understanding, we can see a derivation of a sequent $X \succ Y$ showing how it is that a position in which the members of $X$ are *asserted* and the members of $Y$ are *denied* is self-defeating, or *out of bounds*. Furthermore, we can think of the structural rules as arising out of constraints on assertion and denial as such. For example: IDENTITY expresses the fact that to assert and deny the same thing is out of bounds, WEAKENING is the notion that once a position is out of bounds, adding more assertions and denials does not return the position to the field of play, CONTRACTION tells us that in a position repeated assertion and repeated denial makes no difference – if $A$ is truly asserted in a position, then asserting it

---

[45] See Robert Brandom's *Articulating Reasons* (2000) for an introduction to the distinction between representationalism and inferentialism.

[46] See, for example, (Restall, 2005, 2013; Ripley, 2015a, 2017).

again does not add to what is claimed, and similarly for denial.[47] Finally, CUT tells us that if a position is in bounds, then one of the options: asserting $A$ and denying $A$, at least, will remain in bounds. So, the structural rules have a direct interpretation in terms of norms governing assertion and denial. However, the rules are not all equally accepted. See the discussions of CUT and IDENTITY in the next two sections. They are clearly motivated in terms of the *semantics*, and in what is recognisably about the *rules* for *use* for the vocabulary.

What goes for the structural rules goes also for the connective rules, too. As one example, the derivation of $p, q \lor r \succ p \land q, r$:

$$\frac{\dfrac{p \succ p \quad q \succ q}{p, q \succ p \land q} \land R \qquad r \succ r}{p, q \lor r \succ p \land q, r} \lor L$$

shows how it is that the asserting $p$ and $q \lor r$ and denying $p \land q$ and denying $r$ is out of bounds. That this would be so depends, of course, on the *meanings* of the claims asserted and denied, and in particular, the commitments incurred by asserting $q \lor r$ and by deying $p \land q$. The position $[p, q \lor r : p \land q, r]$ is out of bounds in virtue of the meanings of '$\lor$' and '$\land$'. The left and right rules for the connectives are, on this view, as intimately connected to the meanings of those connectives as the truth conditions for conjunctions and disjunctions are for a representationalist – except here we do not explain those meanings in terms of truth values or models, but in terms of *rules* governing *assertion* and *denial*. In other words, they are suitable for the non-representationalist, especially such a non-representationalist *normative pragmatist*.

On this interpretation of the semantics of the connectives and the significance of the sequent calculus, we can then see *models* as derivative in significance, and not the primary bearers of meaning. A model – in this case, a map from the atoms of the language to $\{0, 1\}$, for classical logic – is an idealisation of any given available position. The completeness argument given in this section is then taken very seriously indeed. A position is a collection of assertions and denials (or, if you like, a possible scoreboard of a given conversation or a *common ground*). A *limit* position, as given by the completeness proof, can be seen as directly arising out of some process of completing a given concrete position into a partition of the language (if we take *Cut* to be present), or a position that is as full as can be, regardless (if not). It is a significant *theorem* that any available position may be embedded in some such ideal completion, and we can see how the idea of a *world*, a decisive evaluation of the language into the *true* and

---

[47] This does not mean that repeated assertion has no effect at all on the 'scoreboard'. Consider a context where $A$ and then $B$ were asserted. Asserting $A$ again changes *what was last asserted*, but it does not change the fact of whether $A$ was granted or not in the conversation. It was.

the *false* can be motivated by, and arise out of, the concrete given practices of assertion and denial. We do not need to start with *worlds* or *valuations* in order to motivate the semantics of classical logic, or of ST. We can start with our concrete practices of assertion and denial and norms governing when such assertions and denials are in or out of bounds.

Or so it might go. The formal *theorems* of completeness and soundness are results connecting two very different ways of understanding language and its significance – its *meaning*. Typically, the philosopher of language takes a stand on the priority of one view over another. The logician is afforded the luxury of not having to take such a stand. The logician's primary role is to map out the kinds of formal and theoretical connections between proofs and models that other philosophers may use in delineating the conceptual priority of the relationship between representationalisms and inferentialisms.

So far we have reflected on the relationship between proofs and models. In the remaining section I will look anew at what our focus on the paradoxes has to add to our reflections on the relationships between proofs and models in philosophical logic.

## 4.2 Paradoxes, Proofs and Models

In this section, we will explore some of the connections between the different philosophical perspectives on proofs and models on the one hand, and our options for the paradoxes, on the other. It is one thing to have (as we have seen in the previous two sections) some technical 'fix' to the paradoxes, asking us to reject this or that inference principle to preserve consistency, or to ward off triviality, at the very least. It is another thing entirely to find some way to *interpret* such a formal account, and to connect the choices made by the formal theory and wider concerns, about truth, about inference and more.

Let's first consider things from the perspective of the representationalist, for whom meaning is to be represented by an interpretation relation, assigning for entities of each syntactic category, objects from the *model*, in which the language is interpreted. Consider first the accounts of the paradoxes in the ballpark of three-valued semantics: $K3$, $LP$, $ST$ and $TS$. In each case, formulas in the language are assigned the values 1, 0 or $n$, with that assignment satisfying the usual conditions for each of the connectives, as is familiar from the previous section. What is less clear is what we should say about why such a tripartite assignment of values is the appropriate one in order to give *semantics* for the vocabulary. A number of options are possible, so let's consider these in turn.

One approach is to say that to assign 1 to a formula is to say that it is *true*, to assign 0 is to say that it is *false*, and to assign $n$ is to say that it is the statement that is not truth apt, or does not express a proposition.[48] On this view, it is clear *why* there are three possible values for sentences, and what the significance of those values amounts to, and why, on such an interpretation, validity might be appropriately understood as preservation of the value 1. There is clearly something worthwhile in keeping track of the preservation of *truth* in this sense. The *K*3 perspective is well founded. If we grant that there are grammatical sentences that fail to enter into the domain of semantic evaluation in the strong sense of having a truth value (and it seems that sentences with presupposition failures are a good candidate for an independent class of such statements, other than the semantic paradoxes), then it is unsurprising that sentences are appropriately modelled in this way and that the familiar connectives have the semantic clauses that are given by the three-valued truth tables.

However, this approach does not, at first blush, answer the question of why there is not *another* connective, like the original negation connective, that sends formulas with either value 0 or value *n* to 1, and formulas with value 1 get sent to 0. There seems to be nothing in the very idea of a sentence receiving value *n* as failing to receive a proper *truth value* that must demand that any negationlike operator *on* such a formula must also result in a formula that lacks a truth value. Yet, if such a 'strong negation' were added to our vocabulary, the liar sentence would return with a vengeance. The defender of such a response to the paradoxes must explain what kinds of operations on truth values are appropriate as semantic values for connectives in our vocabulary, and what operations are out of bounds.

This question becomes starker if we envision our three-valued semantics in a wider setting, say encompassing a range of possible worlds. On the classical two-valued semantic picture, enhanced with worlds, each formula may be interpreted as a function from worlds to truth values, or equivalently, as a set of worlds. Sets of worlds could be understood to be *propositions* in this sense, and a proposition *P* is true (at a world *w*) iff the world *w* is in the set *P*, and it is false otherwise. *Any* set of worlds is, at least potentially, the semantic value some formula (for any such set *P* we may have a formula *A* where *P* = ‖*A*‖, that is, *P* is the set of worlds where *A* holds), and the 'algebra' of all sets of worlds is closed under the familiar operations of intersection (which models conjunction), union (disjunction) and complementation (negation). In any given model of this shape, given by some set of worlds, the set of propositions so defined gives us a 'logical space' on which our language might be interpreted.

Now, let us recast the three-valued semantics in this same light: a proposition is now modelled not by a function from worlds to {0, 1}, or equivalently, by a

---

[48] For one such approach, see Saul Kripke's 'Outline of a Theory of Truth' (1975).

set of worlds, but by a map from worlds to the three values $\{0, n, 1\}$. This is not well modelled by *one* set of worlds.[49] Instead, it would seem better to think of *two* sets of worlds. One way to do this is to think of a proposition as consisting of a pair, $\langle T, F \rangle$, where the sets $T$ and $F$ are disjoint. $T$ is the set of worlds where the proposition is *true* (assigned 1) and $F$ is the set where the proposition is *false* (assigned 0). The propositional connectives have a ready interpretation on this understanding. Given the propositions $\langle T_1, F_1 \rangle$ and $\langle T_2, F_2 \rangle$, their conjunction is $\langle T_1 \cap T_2, F_1 \cup F_2 \rangle$. It is true only in worlds where both conjuncts are true, while it is false wherever both conjuncts are false. The negation of a proposition $\langle T, F \rangle$ is $\langle F, T \rangle$, which seems reasonable enough. However, once we have a space, like this, in which to find propositions, and an independent characterisation of logical relationships between those propositions, new questions arise. If the semantic value of a sentence is a proposition of this kind, then the space of propositions affords *other* operations, which may well be the semantic values of some connectives in our vocabulary. For any proposition $\langle T, F \rangle$ there is another proposition $\langle \overline{T}, T \rangle$ (where $\overline{T}$ is the set of all worlds other than those in $T$), which is *sharp* (it is either true or false *everywhere*) and which is true wherever the original proposition fails to be true, and is false wherever the original proposition is true. Why is *this* not the negation of the original proposition? Or more importantly for our purposes, why does our language not contain an operation that acts like this 'negation', even if it is not the way we should interpret a natural language negation? Is there any *barrier* to the presence of an item in our language that behaves like this? If we take any map from worlds to $\{0, n, 1\}$ to determine a proposition, then for any proposition $\langle T, F \rangle$, there is a unique proposition $\langle \overline{T}, T \rangle$ of just this form. Of course, if there were a sentential operator '$-$' such that if $\|A\| = \langle T, F \rangle$ then $\|-A\| = \langle \overline{T}, T \rangle$, then the liar paradox, in the form of a sentence $\lambda^*$ equivalent to $-T\lambda^*$ would return with a vengeance, because sentences of the form $-T\lambda^*$ receive the value $n$ at no worlds.

So, a representationalist of *this* stripe must rule out operations like this on our space of propositions. One kind of line of response is to say that not *all* of the disjoint pairs of sets of worlds count as possible semantic values for sentences. There is some kind of further constraint on pairs of sets of worlds that means that some pairs $\langle T, F \rangle$ can count as propositions while others do not.[50] I won't

---

[49] Though, we could, of course, understand it as a set of worlds where *membership* is understood in some tripartite way, though this would not be of much use in *modelling* the phenomenon in question.

[50] This is achieved in so-called Routley *star* models for negation by requiring that the set have the form $\langle T, \overline{T^*} \rangle$ for an operator $*$ on worlds. It turns out, in *these* models, that the positive extension $T$ of a sentence *determines* its negative extension, so representationalist semantics that treat negation using the Routley star have some resources to develop a response in this vein (Routley & Routley, 1972; Berto & Restall, 2019).

push the question further here, but there are important questions to ask, because without an answer to them, the response to the semantic paradoxes rings hollow for the representationalist who takes the space defined by the *model* to be, in some sense, the ground of semantic significance and the bearer of meaning. If the underlying space of propositions is structured in a way to allow for the definition of a truth predicate without fear of collapse, that is an impressive result. If the security is found only by a contingent feature of our language (that it does not possess a connective that takes a given semantic value which is, nonetheless 'out there' to be had), then the comfort colder than we might have first thought.

The aforementioned discussion has focussed on *K*3 but can be rephrased for *LP* and *ST* with little change.[51] Regardless of the interpretation in *K*3, *LP* or *ST*, the same issue arises. If in our space of propositions the two components are only weakly tied, and if *any* such pair is a potential semantic value for a sentence, then the field of *propositions* is not itself robustly resistant to collapse in the presence of semantic paradox. We need to supplement our account with some assurance that the language does not (or cannot?) give rise to operators such as the strong negation '−' that would bring collapse. The representationalist needs more resources than three values and the tripartite distinction on worlds induced by those values to be truly *safe*.

> ≺

What can the *inferentialist* say about this issue? Is there any insight to be gained if we start with proofs, rather than models? As we have seen, the inferentialist does not need to take assignments of values to sentences as the starting point for semantics. Perhaps starting with assertion, denial and the bounds will give us different insights into the paradoxes.

We have seen earlier an interpretation of the sequent calculus in terms of norms governing assertion and denial. It proves to be somewhat complicated to interpret these norms as justifying the particular semantic choices of *K*3 and of *LP*, but the connections with *ST* (or *TS*) are quite straightforward. Here, instead of thinking of three different semantic values, we can interpret the language as involving at least two different *standards for application*. Our claims can be

---

[51] For *LP* we can require *T* and *F* to be mutually exhaustive but not necessarily exclusive if we wish the *T* set to collect the worlds at which the proposition is, in some sense true. Then for *LP* propositions, entailment is subsethood of the first component, as for *K*3 propositions. For *ST*, a natural representation for propositions is as a pair $\langle S, T \rangle$ of worlds where the proposition, taken *strictly* holds, and worlds where it holds taken *tolerantly*. The natural requirement is that $S \subseteq T$. For consequence, we note then that $\langle S, T \rangle$ entails $\langle S', T' \rangle$ if $S \subseteq T'$.

taken *strictly* or *tolerantly* (Cobreros et al., 2012). A borderline case of vagueness is the most obvious case. If I point to a borderline case of redness and say '*that's red*' then, strictly speaking, I overstep the mark, while tolerantly speaking, no mistake has been made. Rather than thinking that there are two different *contents* asserted in these two evaluations, we can think of a single claim (to the redness of that object), which is evaluated in a more strict or more tolerant manner in either case. What goes for borderline cases goes, too, for ascriptions of truth, especially in paradoxical cases. Presumably, the wiggle room of borderline cases of vagueness will extend to wiggle room for truth predications of borderline cases too. (After all, what goes for 'that's red' would go for '"that's red" is true' too.) Since predications of truth can vary between strict and tolerant standards, we may also analyse predications of truth in paradoxical cases in this way. It is not implausible to take the liar sentence $\neg T\lambda$ to be at least *tolerantly* true but not *strictly* true, since we have derivations for $\succ \neg T\lambda$ and for $\neg T\lambda \succ$, respectively.[52]

The distinction between strict and tolerant standards for assertion gives us some scope to give an account of the liar paradox, and furthermore, it connects smoothly with the sequent calculus. If we think of sequents as constraining patterns of assertion and denial, then the *ST* calculus is justified by saying that $X \succ Y$ is derivable and only if the *strict* asserition of $X$ and the strict *denial* of $Y$ is out of bounds: or equivalently, if we have a derivation of $A \succ B$ then if we strictly assert $A$, we can justify the *tolerant* assertion of $B$. On this understanding, each of the connective rules has a ready interpretation and justification, and all of the structural rules – other than *Cut* – have justifications at hand. What of *Cut*? This fails, if there is any gap between strict and tolerant assertion (or denial), as it must. We have an independent diagnosis of the failure of *Cut*, on this account, together with a justification of why it seems to us that *Cut* is valid, when we ignore the difference between strict and tolerant standards.

This much works well enough as to an explanation of how it is that *Cut* might fail, and why the traditional derivations of triviality are ruled out. We saw that the representationalist faces wider question concerning the legitimacy of notions that would seem to be definable but which trivialise the theory. The same question arises here: What rules an operator like strong negation out, given an inferentialist understanding of semantics?

If our language were to have an operator like our intended '−', with the target interpretation such that $m(-A) = 0$ iff $m(A) = 1$ and $m(-A) = 1$ otherwise,

---

Égré (2021) makes an extended case for the appropriateness using the notions of tolerant and strict truth for statements like the liar.

then on an *ST*-understanding of these values, $-A$ is strictly deniable (i.e. not tolerantly assertible) if and only if $A$ is strictly assertible, and $-A$ is *strictly* assertible otherwise. So, as expected, there is no gap between strict and tolerant assertibility for $-A$. Could our vocabulary have operators with this behaviour? If lexical items like the putative strong negation acquire their meaning by patterns of use (or rules for use), as the pragmatist holds, and if those are to be encoded by the bounds as expressed formally in the sequent calculus, then we cannot simply impose the intended interpretation by *fiat*. Instead, we must ask how it could be that in any *limit* position, either $-A$ is strictly asserted or $-A$ is strictly denied. We can see how this might be plausible for some special *sharp* contents (such as $\top$ and $\bot$), but for this to hold *in addition* with the constraint that $-A$ is strictly denied in exactly the same limit positions as those in which $\neg A$ is strictly denied (i.e. those in which $A$ is strictly asserted) adds an additional layer of complexity. How might we impose such a constraint on our use of '$-$'? One attempt would be to attempt to go 'up one level' and to internalise into our vocabulary the strict/tolerant distinction and to say that $-A$ says that $A$ is *not tolerantly true*, or equivalently *strictly false*, with the aim that when assessing such an item tolerantly, its status agrees with the tolerant assessment that of $\neg A$, while were we to assess it strictly, its status is unchanged.

While it might be appealing for us to have such an operator in our arsenal, if we have abandoned the argument for *Cut* in its full generality, it is hard to see why it might return here to give us the desired degree of sharpness. This is the standard and well-known problem of higher-order vagueness or revenge paradox. If we thought there was a gap between strict and tolerant standards of assessment of vague terms, then these arguments equally apply to the strict or tolerant assessment of judgements of strict or tolerant truth for those terms. If the truth predicate is paradoxical in such a way as to separate its tolerant truth from its strict truth, then there is no reason to think that this difficulty suddenly disappears when we move up one level.[53] Questions remain, of course, as to what we can or should say about the appropriate rules governing folding in terms of art such as 'determinately' or 'strictly' into our ground-level vocabulary, and what rules might govern such concepts, but the general setting in which the space of semantic evaluation is given by the bounds on positions governed by the structural rules of identity, weakening and contraction, but not *Cut*, seems to be a fruitful space for giving different answers to the question as to how it is that our vocabulary is safe from paradox.

---

[53] Cobreros et al. (2015) discuss some of the issues surrounding such higher-order evaluations, and what this means for *ST*-consequence.

## 4.3 Where to, from Here?

There is much more that could be said, of course, and no doubt, much of it *will* be said in the years ahead. With this section, I will draw this Element to a close. Instead of developing more lines of exploration in the remaining pages, I will point towards what I take to be a number of promising paths for further exploration.

1. We saw in Section 2.3 that CONTRACTION was a prime suspect when it comes to the paradoxes. This is relatively straightfoward *technically* when it comes to proofs and sequent derivations. The significance of rejecting contraction is much less clear when it comes to either the *significance* of proofs and of derivations and norms governing assertion, denial and inference, or the kinds of *models* that might be used to give different insights into how our language represents things as being. Should we expect a relational *worlds* semantics to give insight into how contraction figures into modelling truth, class membership and vague predicates, or should we look for other ways to interpret the different significance of repeated uses of premises in inference? The field is open for further exploration along these lines. Petersen's classic (and sadly neglected) papers are an important reference on the scope for the proof theory (Petersen, 2000, 2003), and the metaphysical considerations in Zardini's (2011) work, in which he offers a proof calculus, may provide grounds for a parallel model-theoretic approach. Standefer's reflections on Zardini's work, though critical, may also inspire new lines of development (Standefer, 2016).

2. What about the rejection of the structural rule of IDENTITY and the concomitant system *TS*? You may think that a calculus in which the IDENTITY axioms are rejected would be simply *empty*, given that derivationds cannot get off the ground. However, the situation with derivable sequents in *TS* parallels precisely the situation with the *tautologies* (formulas evaluated as 1 in every model) in the logic $K3$ (at least, in the language without the constants $\top$ and $\bot$). $K3$ is not a vacuous logic because there are non-vacuous sequents relating $K3$-formulas. The same could be said at one level up in *TS*, given relations between *sequents*. (This approach was first explored by (French, 2016), and (Fjellstand, 2015).) Once we see this, generalisation follows: we could seek to interpret *sequents* in two ways (strictly and tolerantly) and look at *ST* and *TS* relations between sequents, and once the jump is made from 1-sequents to these, higher-order two-sequents, the generalisation to all levels of $\omega$ beckons. This way lies the recent study of *metainferences*, and there is a rich and exciting vein of new research. Start here: (Barrio et al., 2019).

3. In Section 3, I gestured at the relationships between *ST*, *TS*, *LP* and *K*3, to combine transitivity and non-transitivty into one system. If you were temperamentally inclined to *pluralism* about logical consequence (Beall & Restall, 2006), you might welcome the fact that different consequence relations can be defined on the one class of models, and that each pays their way in giving an account of the bounds for assertion and denial. It would be useful to have a general map of the territory here, and to see whether there is a proof-first account of these consequence relations and their interactions. Any further work in this area should consult Ripley's (2015c) examination of different notions of transitivity that are present in systems such as *ST*.

4. I motivated the sequent calculus as arising out of a prior notion of natural deduction *proof*. In the sequent calculus for classical logic, as well as that for *ST* and *TS*, the sequent calculus has left that nursery and is making its own way in the world. It would be fruitful to explore the family connections as well as differences, further, because as mentioned earlier (on page 32) there is a significant open question about the relationship between the rejection of *Cut* and the composition of *proofs*. If I argue: *A* therefore *B*, and so, *C*, on the basis of a proof from *A* to *B* and a proof from *B* to *C* then the one and the same *B* seems to occur both as a conclusion and a premise, and there seems to be *no* equivocation involved between strict and tolerant evaluation of the intermediate formula *B*. How is the sequent calculus, interpreted *ST*-wise, to be related back to proofs? The task remains for the friend of *ST*-consequence to give an account of the relationship between the sequent bounds and an account of natural deduction proof.

5. Our focus has been understanding and relating some of the distinctive accounts of proofs and models inspired and motivated by the paradoxes. The constant between all of the approaches in focus is that they take the paradoxical arguments to require a revision of our standard 'classical' logical framework, and not, instead, a more subtle analysis of the truth predicate, class membership and vague predicates. For an introduction to some more standard classical *axiomatic* theories of truth, consider the books by (Halbach, 2011) and (Horsten, 2011), and for a model-theoretic approach that takes the truth predicate to invoke a *revision* from one model to another, the monograph by Gupta & Belnap (1993) is the place to start, and then recent articles expand the basic revision approach with a *modal*-inspired way to interpret the revision rule into the object-language (Standefer, 2015; Gupta & Standefer, 2017, 2018). See particularly (Standefer, 2016), which relates the rejection of contraction with the revision theory.

6. Finally, there is more work to be done in exploring the relationship between proofs and models for modal and quantificational vocabulary. The

current defence of necessitism (the view that everything that exists, exists necessarily) is motivated by the simplicity and power of the modal model theory (Williamson, 2013). There is no doubt that modal models are rich and powerful. However, further options seem open to consider the proof-first accounts of modal logic that connect smoothly with the speech acts in use in modal discourse, such as *supposing*, in the different senses of this word (Lance & White, 2007; Restall, 2012), and similarly, accounts of singular terms and quantification in vocabularies where we may not simply take as given that each singular term has a referent (Feferman, 1995; Restall, 2019). The line sketched out here concerning the relationship between proofs and models will, I think, give us better tools to understand the power and significance of possible worlds models and their connection to our everyday practices.

# Glossary of Symbols

$\rightarrow$ The *conditional*: A two-place connective. If $A$ and $B$ are formulas, then so is $A \rightarrow B$, the conditional, with antecedent $A$ and consequent $B$, which can be read as 'if $A$ then $B$'.

$\implies$ The *rule separator* in a Hilbert proof system: The rule of *modus ponens* is written in the form '$A \rightarrow B, A \implies B$', which means that in a Hilbert proof, we can write '$B$' on a line if we have previously written '$A \rightarrow B$' and '$A$' on earlier lines.

$\wedge$ *Conjunction*: A two-place connective. If $A$ and $B$ are formulas, then so is $A \wedge B$, the conjunction, with $A$ and $B$ as conjuncts. It can be read: '$A$ and $B$'.

$\vee$ *Disjunction*: A two-place connective. If $A$ and $B$ are formulas, then so is $A \vee B$, the disjunction, with $A$ and $B$ as disjuncts. It can be read: '$A$ or $B$'. Disjunction in the systems considered here is invariably understood *inclusively*: if $p \vee q$ holds, this does not exclude the possibility of both $p$ and $q$ holding together.

$\neg$ *Negation*: A one-place connective. If $A$ is a formula, then so is $\neg A$, its negation, with $A$ as its *negand*. It can be read: 'it is not the case that $A$', or more simply 'not $A$'.

$\forall$ The *universal quantifier*: If $A(x)$ is a formula and $x$ is a variable, then $\forall x A(x)$ is a formula, which states that every object $t$ is such that $A(t)$ holds.

$\exists$ The *existential quantifier*: If $A(x)$ is a formula and $x$ is a variable, then $\exists x A(x)$ is a formula, which states that some object $t$ is such that $A(t)$ holds.

$\perp$ The *falsum*: a propositional *constant*. The formula $\perp$ is, by convention, false.

( ) *Parentheses*: used in formulas to fix the scopes of connectives and quantifiers. The formula $A \wedge (B \vee C)$ is the conjunction of $A$ with $B \vee C$, while the formula $(A \wedge B) \vee C$ is the disjunction of $A \vee B$ with $C$. '$A \wedge B \vee C$', without any parentheses, is ambiguous between these two readings, unless some precedence is established between $\wedge$ and $\vee$, or some preference is given to associating towards the left or towards the right. No such conventions are in place in this *Element*, and we always use parentheses to disambiguate formulas where necessary.

= The *identity predicate*: A two-place predicate, where $s = t$ states that the objects $s$ and $t$ are *the same thing*.

≠ The *negated* identity predicate: '$s \neq t$' is a conventional way to write the negation of the formula $s = t$.

Π A *proof*. The notation is used when we wish to talk about proofs in general. For example, if Π is a proof of a conjunction $A \wedge B$, then by extending Π with one $\wedge E$ step, we have a proof from the same premises as Π but now to the conclusion $A$.

[ ] *Discharge brackets*: Used in proofs to mark the discharge of an assumption. Almost invariably flagged with a superscript, indicating the step in the proof at which the assumption was discharged.

⌜ ⌝ *Corner quotes*: Used to convert *formulas* to *singular terms*. If $A$ is a formula, then $\ulcorner A \urcorner$ is a singular term. So, the formula '$\ulcorner A \urcorner = \ulcorner B \urcorner$' states that the formulas $A$ and $B$ are *the same formula*.

$T$ The *truth* predicate: $Tx$ states that the object $x$ is *true*. Typically used with corner quotes, so that the claim that the sentence $A$ is true has the form $T\ulcorner A \urcorner$.

∈ (also ∉) The *membership* predicate for sets, and its negation: $s \in t$ states that the object $s$ (perhaps a set, perhaps not) is a member of the set $t$. To say that $s \notin t$ is to say that $s$ is *not* a member of $t$.

⤳ The *one-step reduction* relation on proofs: $\Pi \rightsquigarrow \Pi'$ holds if there is one reduction step transforming Π into Π'.

{ : } The *set-forming* abstractor: If $A(x)$ is some formula, in which the variable $x$ may occur free, the term '$\{x : A(x)\}$' is a singular term, used to denote the set of all objects $t$ such that $A(t)$ holds.

≻ The *sequent-separator* turnstile: If $X$ is some collection of formulas (possibly a set, possibly a multiset, possibly a list – and possibly empty), and $A$ is a formula, then the *sequent* $X \succ A$ represents the argument *from* the premises $X$ to the conclusion $A$. Sequents may be valid or invalid. Sometimes we allow for sequents to have collections on the conclusion side as well. Sequents of the form $X \succ Y$ are called *multiple-conclusion* sequents.

⊢ (also ⊬) The *provability* turnstile (and its negation): We write '$X \vdash A$' to say that there is a proof of $A$ from $X$, or equivalently, a proof for the sequent $X \succ A$. We also use this notation in the multiple-conclusion setting, writing '$X \vdash Y$' to say that there is a derivation of the sequent $X \succ Y$. As usual, we slash this turnstile, writing '$\nvdash$' to say that there is no such proof (or derivation). Sometimes the turnstile is decorated with a subscript, where $\vdash_S$ states that there is a proof *in system S*.

$\lambda$ A *singular term*: $\lambda$ is most often used to refer to a *liar* sentence, some object $\lambda$ where $\lambda = \ulcorner \neg T\lambda \urcorner$. That is, some sentence such that it is *identical* to the sentence that says that it is not true.

$\square$ *Necessity*: A one-place connective, a modal operator. If $A$ is a formula, then so is $\square A$. It can be read: 'it is necessary that $A$'.

$\lozenge$ *Possibility*: A one-place connective, a modal operator. If $A$ is a formula, then so is $\square A$. IT can be read as 'it is possible that $A$'.

$\Rightarrow$ The *strict conditional*: A two-place connective, a modalised conditional. If $A$ and $B$ are formulas, so is $A \Rightarrow B$, which states that it is *necessary* that a

$\Vdash$ (also $\nVdash$) The *supports* relation: holds between some object at which formulas may be evaluated (a valuation, a model, a world) and a formula. We write '$x \Vdash A$' to say that $A$ is true at (or according to) $x$, and $x \nVdash A$' to say that $A$ is not true at (or according to) $x$.

$\Vdash^+$ (also $\nVdash^+$) The *supervaluational* supports relation: holds between some *set* of objects at which formulas may be evaluated (valuations, models, worlds) and a formula. We write '$s \Vdash^+ A$' to say that $x \Vdash A$ for every $x \in s$, and '$s \nVdash^+ A$' to say that it is not the case that $x \Vdash A$ for every $x \in s$, or equivalently, that there is some $x \in s$ where $x \nVdash A$.

$\vDash$ (also $\nvDash$, and also with subscripts) The *validity* turnstile (and its negation): We write '$X \vDash A$' to say that there is no counterexample to the argument from $X$ to $A$. That is, (variously) there is no (valuation, world, model) at which every member of $X$ holds, but $A$ doesn't. The definition can extend to multiple-conclusion sequents in a natural way: $X \vDash Y$ holds if and only if there is no (valuation, world, model) at which every member of $X$ holds and every member of $Y$ fails to hold. Sometimes annotated with a subscript: we write '$X \vDash_S Y$' to say that there is the argument from $X$ to $Y$ is valid *in system S*.

$\sqsubseteq$ (also $\subseteq$): *Partial order relations*: A *reflexive partial order*, such as $\sqsubseteq$ is a two-place relation that is transitive (if $x \sqsubseteq y$ and $y \sqsubseteq z$ then $x \sqsubseteq z$, for each $x, y, z$), *reflexive* ($x \sqsubseteq x$ for every $x$) and *asymmetric* (if $x \sqsubseteq y$ and $y \sqsubseteq x$ then $x = y$, for each $x, y$). An *irreflexive partial order* (like $\sqsubset$) is *transitive, irreflexive* ($x \not\sqsubset x$, for each $x$) and *anti-symmetric* (if $x \sqsubset y$ then $y \not\sqsubset x$). For any irreflexive partial order $\sqsubset$, we can define a reflexive partial order $\sqsubseteq$ by setting $x \sqsubseteq y$ iff either $x \sqsubset y$ or $x = y$. Conversely, given a reflexive partial order $\sqsubseteq$, we can define an irreflexive partial order $\sqsubset$ by setting $x \sqsubset y$ iff both $x \sqsubseteq y$ and $x \neq y$.

$\omega$ The set of all *natural numbers*: $\omega$ is the smallest set such that $0 \in \omega$ and whenever $n \in \omega$ then $n + 1 \in \omega$ too.

$\langle\,,\,\rangle$ The notation for an *ordered pair*. For any objects $x$ and $y$, $\langle x,y \rangle$ is the pair, with $x$ as its first element and $y$ as its second. Ordered pairs are *ordered*: The pair $\langle 0,1 \rangle$ is not the same as the pair $\langle 1,0 \rangle$.

$[\;:\;]$ A *position*: If $X$ and $Y$ are sets of formulas, $[X:Y]$ is a *position*, according to which every member $X$ holds and every member of $Y$ fails. A position is said to be *available* when $X \nvdash Y$.

$\subseteq$ The *subset* relation: $s \subseteq t$ holds if and only if every member of $s$ is also a member of $t$.

$\cup$ Set *union* for a pair of sets: if $s$ and $t$ are sets, then $s \cup t$ is the set consisting of every object that is *either* a member of $s$, *or* a member of $t$.

$\cap$ Set *intersection* for a pair of sets: if $s$ and $t$ are sets, then $s \cap t$ is the set consisting of every object that is *both* a member of $s$, *and* a member of $t$.

$\bigcup$ Set *union* for an arbitrary collection of sets: If $S$ is a set of sets, then $\bigcup S$ is the set containing all and only those things that are members of *some* member of $S$. If $S = \{X_n : n \in \omega\}$, we also write $\bigcup_{n=0}^{\infty} X_n$ for $\bigcup S$, the union of each of the sets $X_n$.

$\bigcap$ Set *intersection* for an arbitrary collection of sets: If $S$ is a set of sets, then $\bigcap S$ is the set containing all and only those things that are members of *every* member of $S$. If $T = \{X_n : n \in \omega\}$, we also write $\bigcap_{n=0}^{\infty} X_n$ for $\bigcap T$, the intersection of each of the sets $X_n$.

$\|\;\|$ The *extension* of a formula in a model. If $A$ is a formula evaluated in a worlds model, $\|A\|$ is the set of all worlds at which $A$ holds.

# References

Barrio, E., Rosenblatt, L., & Tajer, D. (2014). The logics of strict-tolerant logic. *Journal of Philosophical Logic*, 44(5), 551–571.

Barrio, E. A., Pailos, F., & Szmuc, D. (2019). (Meta)inferential levels of entailment beyond the Tarskian paradigm. *Synthese*. Online first.

Beall, J. et al. (2012). On the ternary relation and conditionality. *Journal of Philosophical Logic*, 41(3), 595–612.

Beall, J. & Restall, G. (2006). *Logical Pluralism*. Oxford: Oxford University Press.

Beall, J. & van Fraassen, B. (2003). *Possibilities and Paradox: An Introduction to Modal and Many-Valued Logic*. Oxford: Oxford University Press.

Belnap, N. D. (1962). Tonk, plonk and plink. *Analysis*, 22, 130–134.

Belnap, N. D. (1977a). How a computer should think. In G. Ryle (ed.), *Contemporary Aspects of Philosophy* (pp. 30–55). Boston: Oriel Press.

Belnap, N. D. (1977b). A useful four-valued logic. In J. Dunn & G. Epstein (eds.), *Modern Uses of Multiple-Valued Logics* (pp. 8–37). Dordrecht: Reidel.

Berto, F. & Restall, G. (2019). Negation on the Australian plan. *Journal of Philosophical Logic*, 48(6), 1119–1144.

Blackburn, P., de Rijke, M., & Venema, Y. (2001). *Modal Logic*. Cambridge University Press.

Blamey, S. (1986). Partial logic. In D. Gabbay & F. Guenthner (eds.), *Handbook of Philosophical Logic*, volume III (pp. 261–353). Dordrecht: D. Reidel.

Brady, R. T. (1971). The consistency of the axioms of abstraction and extensionality in a three-valued logic. *Notre Dame Journal of Formal Logic*, 12, 447–453.

Brandom, R. (1983). Asserting. *Noûs*, 17(4), 637–650.

Brandom, R. B. (2000). *Articulating Reasons: An Introduction to Inferentialism*. Cambridge, MA: Harvard University Press.

Brouwer, L. E. J. (1913). Intuitionism and formalism. *Bulletin of the American Mathematical Society*, 20, 91–96. Reprinted as Brouwer (1999).

Brouwer, L. E. J. (1999). Intuitionism and formalism. *Bulletin of the American Mathematical Society*, 37(1), 55–64. Reprint of Brouwer (1913).

Carroll, L. (1895). What the Tortoise said to Achilles. *Mind*, 4(14), 278–280.

Chellas, B. F. (1980). *Modal Logic: An Introduction*. Cambridge: Cambridge University Press.

Cobreros, P., Egré, P., Ripley, D., & van Rooij, R. (2012). Tolerant, classical, strict. *Journal of Philosophical Logic*, 41(2), 347–385.

Cobreros, P., Egré, P., Ripley, D., & van Rooij, R. (2015). Vagueness, truth and permissive consequence. In T. Achourioti, H. Galinon, J. Martínez Fernández, & K. Fujimoto (eds.), *Unifying the Philosophy of Truth* (pp. 409–430). Dordrecht: Springer Netherlands.

Coffa, J. A. (1993). *The Semantic Tradition from Kant to Carnap*. Cambridge, UK: Cambridge University Press. Edited by Linda Wessels.

Copeland, B. (1983). Pure semantics and applied semantics. *Topoi*, 2, 197–204.

Copeland, B. J. (1979). On when a semantics is not a semantics: some reasons for disliking the Routley-Meyer semantics for relevance logic. *Journal of Philosophical Logic*, 8(1), 399–413.

Dummett, M. (1977). *Elements of Intuitionism*. Oxford: Oxford University Press.

Dunn, J. M. (1976). Intuitive semantics for first-degree entailments and 'coupled trees'. *Philosophical Studies*, 29(3), 149–168.

Dunn, J. M. (2000). Partiality and its dual. *Studia Logica*, 65, 5–40.

Dunn, J. M. & Restall, G. (2002). Relevance logic. In D. M. Gabbay (ed.), *Handbook of Philosophical Logic*, volume 6 (pp. 1–136). Dordrecht: Kluwer Academic Publishers, second edition.

Égré, P. (2021). Half-truths and the liar. In C. Nicolai & J. Stern (eds.), *Modes of Truth: The Unified Approach to Truth, Modality and Paradox* (pp. 18–40). London: Routledge.

Feferman, S. (1995). Definedness. *Erkenntnis*, 43(3), 295–320.

Fjellstand, A. (2015). How a semantics for tonk should be. *The Review of Symbolic Logic*, 8(3), 488–505.

French, R. (2016). Structural reflexivity and the paradoxes of self-reference. *Ergo, an Open Access Journal of Philosophy*, 3, 113–31.

French, R. & Ripley, D. (2018). Valuations: Bi, tri, and tetra. *Studia Logica*, 107(6), 1313–1346.

Gamut, L. T. F. (1991). *Logic, Language, and Meaning: Volume 2, Intensional Logic and Logical Grammar*. Chicago: University of Chicago Press.

Genesereth, M. & Kao, E. J. (2016). *Introduction to Logic*. Morgan & Claypool Publishers LLC.

Gentzen, G. (1935a). Untersuchungen über das logische schließen. I. *Mathematische Zeitschrift*, 39(1), 176–210.

Gentzen, G. (1935b). Untersuchungen über das logische schließen. II. *Mathematische Zeitschrift*, 39(1), 405–431.

Gentzen, G. (1969). *The Collected Papers of Gerhard Gentzen*. Amsterdam: North Holland.

Gilmore, P. C. (1974). The consistency of partial set theory without extensionality. In Dana S. Scott (ed.), *Axiomatic Set Theory*, volume 13 of *Proceedings of Symposia in Pure Mathematics* (pp. 147–153). Providence, Rhode Island: American Mathematical Society.

Gupta, A. & Belnap, N. (1993). *The Revision Theory of Truth*. Cambridge, MA: MIT Press.

Gupta, A. & Standefer, S. (2017). Conditionals in theories of truth. *Journal of Philosophical Logic*, 46, 27–63.

Gupta, A. & Standefer, S. (2018). Intersubstitutivity principles and the generalization function of truth. *Synthese*, 195(3), 1065–1075.

Halbach, V. (2011). *Axiomatic Theories of Truth*. Cambridge, UK: Cambridge University Press.

Horsten, L. (2011). *The Tarskian Turn: Deflationism and Axiomatic Truth*. Cambridge, MA: The MIT Press.

Hughes, G. & Cresswell, M. (1996). *A New Introduction to Modal Logic*. London: Routledge.

Kleene, S. C. (1950). *Introduction to Metamathematics*. Princeton: D. van Nostrand.

Kripke, S. (1975). Outline of a theory of truth. *The Journal of Philosophy*, 72(19), 690–716.

Lackey, J. (2007). Norms of assertion. *Noûs*, 41(4), 594–626.

Lance, M. & White, W. H. (2007). Stereoscopic vision: Persons, freedom, and two spaces of material inference. *Philosophers' Imprint*, 7(4), 1–21.

Martin, R. L. & Woodruff, P. W. (1975). On representing 'true-in-$L$' in $L$. *Philosophia (Israel)*, 5, 213–217.

Milne, P. (2002). Harmony, purity, simplicity and a 'seemingly magical fact'. *Monist*, 85(4), 498–534.

Pelletier, F. J. (1999). A brief history of natural deduction. *History and Philosophy of Logic*, 20(1), 1–31.

Petersen, U. (2000). Logic without contraction as based on inclusion and unrestricted abstraction. *Studia Logica*, 64(3), 365–403.

Petersen, U. (2003). $L^i D_\lambda^Z$ as a basis for PRA. *Archive for Mathematical Logic*, 42(7), 665–694.

Poggiolesi, F. (2008). A cut-free simple sequent calculus for modal logic s5. *Review of Symbolic Logic*, 1, 3–15.

Poggiolesi, F. (2009). The method of tree-hypersequents for modal propositional logic. In D. Makinson, J. Malinowski, & H. Wansing (eds.), *Towards Mathematical Philosophy*, volume 28 (pp. 31–51). Dordrecht: Springer Netherlands.

Poggiolesi, F. (2010). *Gentzen Calculi for Modal Propositional Logic*. Trends in Logic. Dordrecht: Springer.

Poggiolesi, F. & Restall, G. (2012). Interpreting and applying proof theories for modal logic. In G. Restall & G. Russell (eds.), *New Waves in Philosophical Logic* (pp. 39–62). Basingstoke, UK: Palgrave Macmillan.

Prawitz, D. (1965). *Natural Deduction: A Proof Theoretical Study*. Stockholm: Almqvist and Wiksell.

Prawitz, D. (1973). Towards a foundation of general proof theory. In P. Suppes, L. Henkin, A. Joja, & G. C. Moisil (eds.), *Logic, Methodology and Philosophy of Science IV* (pp. 225–250). Amsterdam: North Holland.

Prawitz, D. (1974). On the idea of a general proof theory. *Synthese*, 27, 63–77.

Prawitz, D. (2019). The fundamental problem of general proof theory. *Studia Logica*, 107(1), 11–29.

Priest, G. (1979). The logic of paradox. *Journal of Philosophical Logic*, 8(1), 219–241.

Prior, A. N. (1960). The runabout inference-ticket. *Analysis*, 21(2), 38–39.

Read, S. (2008). Harmony and modality. In C. Dégremont, L. Kieff, & H. Rückert (eds.), *Dialogues, Logics and Other Strange Things: Essays in Honour of Shahid Rahman* (pp. 285–303). London: College Publications.

Read, S. (2015). Semantic pollution and syntactic purity. *The Review of Symbolic Logic*, 8(4), 649–661.

Restall, G. (2000). *An Introduction to Substructural Logics*. London: Routledge.

Restall, G. (2005). Multiple conclusions. In P. Hájek, L. Valdés-Villanueva, & D. Westerståhl (eds.), *Logic, Methodology and Philosophy of Science: Proceedings of the Twelfth International Congress* (pp. 189–205). London: KCL Publications.

Restall, G. (2009). Truth values and proof theory. *Studia Logica*, 92(2), 241–264.

Restall, G. (2012). A cut-free sequent system for two-dimensional modal logic, and why it matters. *Annals of Pure and Applied Logic*, 163(11), 1611–1623.

Restall, G. (2013). Assertion, denial and non-classical theories. In K. Tanaka, F. Berto, E. Mares, & F. Paoli (eds.), *Paraconsistency: Logic and Applications* (pp. 81–99). Dordrecht: Springer.

Restall, G. (2014). Pluralism and proofs. *Erkenntnis*, 79(2), 279–291.

Restall, G. (2019). Generality and existence 1: Quantification and free logic. *Review of Symbolic Logic*, 12, 1–29.

Restall, G. & Standefer, S. (2021). Collection frames for substructural logics. Paper in progress.

Restall, G. & Standefer, S. (2022). *Logical Methods*. Cambridge, MA: MIT Press. In press.

Ripley, D. (2011). Contradictions at the borders. In R. Nouwen, R. van Rooij, U. Sauerland, & H.-C. Schmitz (eds.), *Vagueness in Communication* (pp. 169–188). Berlin, Heidelberg: Springer Berlin Heidelberg.

Ripley, D. (2015a). Anything goes. *Topoi*, 34(1), 25–36.

Ripley, D. (2015b). Comparing substructural theories of truth. *Ergo, an Open Access Journal of Philosophy*, 2(20190926), 299–328.

Ripley, D. (2015c). 'Transitivity' of consequence relations. In W. van der Hoek, W. Holliday, & W. Wang (eds.), *Logic, Rationality, and Interaction* (pp. 328–340). Berlin, Heidelberg: Springer Berlin Heidelberg.

Ripley, D. (2017). Bilateralism, coherence, warrant. In F. Moltmann & M. Textor (eds.), *Act-Based Conceptions of Propositional Content* (pp. 307–324). Oxford: Oxford University Press.

Routley, R. & Meyer, R. K. (1973). Semantics of entailment. In H. Leblanc (Ed.), *Truth, Syntax and Modality* (pp. 194–243). North Holland. Proceedings of the Temple University Conference on Alternative Semantics.

Routley, R. & Routley, V. (1972). Semantics of first degree entailment. *Noûs*, 6(4), 335–359.

Sher, G. (1991). *The Bounds of Logic*. Cambridge, MA: MIT Press.

Sider, T. (2010). *Logic for Philosophy*. Oxford: Oxford University Press.

Sieg, W. (2013). *Hilbert's Programs and Beyond*. New York: Oxford University Press.

Smullyan, R. M. (1968). *First-Order Logic*. Berlin: Springer-Verlag Reprinted by Dover Press, 1995.

Standefer, S. (2015). Solovay-type theorems for circular definitions. *The Review of Symbolic Logic*, 8(3), 467–487.

Standefer, S. (2016). Contraction and revision. *The Australasian Journal of Logic*, 13(3), 58–77.

Steinberger, F. (2011). Why conclusions should remain single. *Journal of Philosophical Logic*, 40(3), 333–355.

Stevenson, J. T. (1961). Roundabout the runabout inference-ticket. *Analysis*, 21(6), 124–128.

Van Dalen, D. (1986). Intuitionistic logic. In D. Gabbay & F. Guenthner (eds.), *Handbook of Philosophical Logic*, volume III (pp. 225–339). Dordrecht: D. Reidel.

Von Plato, J. (2001). Natural deduction with general elimination rules. *Archive for Mathematical Logic*, 40, 541–567.

Williamson, T. (2013). *Modal Logic as Metaphysics*. Oxford: Oxford University Press.

Zach, R. (1999). Completeness before Post: Bernays, Hilbert, and the development of propositional logic. *Bulletin of Symbolic Logic*, 5(3), 331–366.

Zach, R. (2019). Hilbert's Program. In E. N. Zalta (ed.), *The Stanford Encyclopedia of Philosophy*. Metaphysics Research Lab, Stanford, CA: Stanford University, Fall 2019 edition.

Zardini, E. (2011). Truth without contra(di)ction. *The Review of Symbolic Logic*, 4(4), 498–535.

# Acknowledgements

As I write this Element, I am in the final stages of making the transition from the University of Melbourne to the University of St Andrews, so, while these pages do not have enough space to acknowledge all my debts, I would like to name just a few who have made it possible to write this Element while preparing to move from one side of the world to the other. Thanks to Shawn Standefer, my colleague, co-author and friend, for shaping my thinking, for asking tough questions, and for being a willing conversation partner. Thanks are due to Rohan French and to two anonymous referees of the Element, who gave me useful feedback on drafts at various stages of writing. Finally, I would especially like to thank my Wednesday lunchtime crew of research students at Melbourne over the last few years – Adam, John, Kai, Lian, Saki and Timo – for their encouragement, feedback, enthusiasm and patience as I attempted to place this Element in its wider philosophical context. If this Element succeeds in its aim to help philosophers (and others) understand some of the shape and significance of current research in philosophical logic, each of you will have played no small part in that.

# About the Author

Greg Restall is Shelby Cullom Davis Professor of Philosophy at the University of St Andrews. He received his PhD from the University of Queensland in 1994. His research focuses on logic and language. His research has been funded by the Australian Research Council, and he is a Fellow of the Australian Academy of the Humanities. Further details of his research can be found at his website: https://consequently.org/

Cambridge Elements

# Philosophy and Logic

## Bradley Armour-Garb
### SUNY Albany

Brad Armour-Garb is chair and Professor of Philosophy at SUNY Albany. His books include *The Law of Non-Contradiction* (co-edited with Graham Priest and J. C. Beall, 2004), *Deflationary Truth and Deflationism and Paradox* (both co-edited with J. C. Beall, 2005), *Pretense and Pathology* (with James Woodbridge, Cambridge University Press, 2015), *Reflections on the Liar* (2017), and *Fictionalism in Philosophy* (co-edited with Fred Kroon, 2020).

## Frederick Kroon
### The University of Auckland

Frederick Kroon is Emeritus Professor of Philosophy at the University of Auckland. He has authored numerous papers in formal and philosophical logic, ethics, philosophy of language, and metaphysics, and is the author of *A Critical Introduction to Fictionalism* (with Stuart Brock and Jonathan McKeown-Green, 2018).

## About the Series

This Cambridge Elements series provides an extensive overview of the many and varied connections between philosophy and logic. Distinguished authors provide an up-to-date summary of the results of current research in their fields and give their own take on what they believe are the most significant debates influencing research, drawing original conclusions.

Cambridge Elements $^{\equiv}$

# Philosophy and Logic

Printed in the United States
by Baker & Taylor Publisher Services